FLUID MECHANICS AND HYDRAULIC MACHINE

DAINIKKUMAR VASANTBHAI SAVALIA

To my beloved mother, Smt. Bhanuben, whose unwavering love, sacrifices, and silent strength have laid the foundation of every step I have taken.

To my students, whose curiosity and hunger for knowledge have inspired the pages of this book. This work is a tribute to your learning journey — may it guide and support you through the challenges of Fluid Mechanics and Hydraulic Machines.

To my mentors and colleagues, for their constant guidance, motivation, and encouragement throughout my academic and research career.

And finally, to the noble pursuit of knowledge — may this book serve as a small contribution to the world of engineering education.

Contents

Foreword

As a teacher and learner of mechanical engineering, I have seen many students struggle with the subjects of Fluid Mechanics and Hydraulic Machines. The concepts often seem too theoretical or complex, especially for diploma-level students who are just starting to connect engineering theory with practical applications.

This book has been written with one simple aim — to make learning easier, more interesting, and more useful for students. Every topic has been explained in a step-by-step manner using simple language, clear definitions, and relevant examples. I have included solved numerical problems, practical applications, and key points to help students understand and remember important concepts.

The content of this book closely follows the diploma mechanical engineering syllabus and is designed to be a helpful companion both in the classroom and during self-study. My focus throughout has been on clarity, simplicity, and usefulness.

I hope that this book becomes a valuable tool for students, helping them not only pass exams but also develop a genuine understanding of how fluid systems and machines work in the real world.

— Dainikkumar Vasantbhai Savalia
Assistant Professor, PIET-DS
Parul University, Vadodara

Preface

This book, Fluid Mechanics and Hydraulic Machines, is written especially for diploma students of mechanical engineering. Over the years, while teaching this subject, I noticed that many students find it difficult to understand because of complex terms, formulas, and theory-heavy textbooks. This motivated me to create a book that explains every concept in a simple, clear, and engaging way.

The main goal of this book is to help students build a strong foundation in fluid mechanics and hydraulic machines. The topics are arranged exactly as per the syllabus, starting from the basic properties of fluids to advanced topics like turbines and pumps. I have explained each concept step by step, used real-life examples, and included solved numerical problems wherever necessary.

I believe that this book will not only help students perform well in exams but also give them a better understanding of practical applications in industries like power plants, water supply systems, and hydraulic machinery.

I sincerely hope that students find this book helpful and enjoyable. I welcome feedback and suggestions to improve future editions.

— Dainikkumar Vasantbhai Savalia

Assistant Professor, PIET-DS

Parul University, Vadodara

Acknowledgements

Writing this book has been a rewarding journey, and I am grateful to many individuals who supported and encouraged me along the way.

First and foremost, I would like to express my sincere thanks to Parul Institute of Engineering and Technology – Diploma Studies (PIET-DS), Parul University, Vadodara, for providing an excellent academic environment and constant motivation to contribute to student learning.

I am deeply thankful to my colleagues, mentors, and friends in the Mechanical Engineering Department for their valuable inputs, suggestions, and encouragement throughout this process.

Special thanks to my students, whose curiosity and questions inspired me to simplify concepts and create a book that truly supports learning at the diploma level.

I would also like to thank Notion Press for offering this wonderful platform to share my work with a wider audience and for their guidance throughout the publication process.

Last but not least, I extend my heartfelt gratitude to my family for their patience, support, and belief in me during this journey.

— Dainikkumar Vasantbhai Savalia
Assistant Professor, PIET-DS
Parul University, Vadodara

Prologue

Fluid Mechanics and Hydraulic Machines play a significant role in the world around us, from the water we drink to the energy that powers our homes. The principles of fluid flow, pressure, and energy conversion form the backbone of many industries, including power generation, transportation, and manufacturing.

As students, it might be difficult to immediately see how the abstract concepts you learn in this subject apply to real-life situations. However, by mastering the basics, you will unlock the ability to understand and solve engineering challenges that impact daily life. Whether it's designing efficient pumps, optimizing energy systems, or ensuring safe and reliable hydraulic machinery, the knowledge you gain here will be indispensable.

This book was written with the goal of simplifying these complex concepts and making them accessible to students pursuing diploma studies in mechanical engineering. Through clear explanations, worked-out examples, and a focus on practical applications, I hope to inspire a deeper interest in the subject and make learning more engaging.

I invite you to explore the chapters, solve the problems, and see how these fundamental principles shape the world of engineering.

CHAPTER ONE

PROPERTIES OF FLUIDS AND PRESSURE MEASUREMENT

1.1 Introduction to Fluids

Fluids are substances that continuously deform (flow) under the action of an applied force. They include both liquids (e.g., water, oil) and gases (e.g., air, steam). Unlike solids, which have a fixed shape, fluids take the shape of the container they occupy. Understanding the behavior of fluids is essential for engineering, particularly in areas like hydraulics, aerodynamics, and power generation.

In this chapter, we will explore the various properties of fluids, such as density, viscosity, and surface tension, that help engineers understand fluid behavior and design efficient systems.

1.2 Properties of Fluids

1.2.1 Density (ρ)

Density is the mass of a fluid per unit volume. It is an important property because it affects how fluids behave under various conditions and influences the design of fluid systems. The formula for density is:

$$\rho = \frac{Volume}{Mass} \left({}^{kg}\!/_{m^3} \right)$$

SI Unit : kg/m3

The density of fluids varies with temperature and pressure. Here are some examples of the density of common fluids:

Water at 4°C: 1000 kg/m³

Air at 20°C: 1.225 kg/m³

Mercury at 20°C: 13,600 kg/m³

Oil (typical): 800–900 kg/m³

As you can see, different fluids have widely varying densities, and this difference is crucial when designing systems that involve fluid flow (e.g., pipes, pumps, and turbines).

1.2.2 Specific Gravity (S)

Specific Gravity is the ratio of the density of a fluid to the density of water at 4°C (which is 1000 kg/m³). It is a dimensionless quantity, meaning it has no units. Specific gravity is useful for comparing the densities of different fluids.

$$S = \frac{Density\ of\ fliud}{Density\ of\ water\ at\ 4°C}$$

Dimensionless quantity

For example:

Water: SG = 1000/1000=1

Mercury: SG = 13600/1000=13.6

Oil: SG = 850/1000=0.85

Since the density of water is used as the reference, specific gravity gives you an idea of whether a fluid is denser (SG > 1) or lighter (SG < 1) than water.

1.2.3 Specific Weight (γ)

Specific Weight is the weight of a fluid per unit volume and is directly related to the density of the fluid. It is calculated by multiplying the fluid's density by the acceleration due to gravity.

$$\gamma = \rho \times g \ (N/m^3)$$

SI Unit : N/m3

For water at 4°C:
γ = 1000 kg/m3 × 9.81 m/s2 = 9810 N/m3
Specific weight is often used in applications where the gravitational force plays a key role, such as in fluid statics and the design of structures that interact with fluids.

1.2.4 Specific Volume (v)

Specific Volume is the inverse of density and is defined as the volume occupied by a unit mass of fluid. It is useful for understanding the space that a given mass of fluid will occupy.

$$v = \frac{1}{\rho} \left(\frac{m^3}{kg} \right)$$

SI Unit : m3/kg

For example, the specific volume of water at 4°C is:
v = 1/1000 = 0.001 m3/kg

Since fluids with lower density will have a higher specific volume, this property helps when designing systems that require fluid storage or flow measurement.

1.2.5 Dynamic Viscosity (μ)

Dynamic Viscosity is a measure of a fluid's resistance to flow. It represents the internal friction between layers of the fluid as they move past each other. Fluids with high viscosity flow slowly (e.g., honey), while fluids with low viscosity flow easily (e.g., water).

The formula for dynamic viscosity is:

$$\mu = \frac{\text{Shear stress}}{\text{Shear rate}}$$

SI Unit : Pa·s or N·s\m2

For water at 20°C, the dynamic viscosity is approximately $1.002 \times 10{-3}$ N·s\m2. For glycerin, it is much higher around 1.49 N·s\m2.

1.2.6 Kinematic Viscosity (v)

Kinematic Viscosity is the ratio of dynamic viscosity to the fluid's density. It helps quantify how a fluid behaves when moving under the influence of gravity.

$$v = \frac{\rho}{\mu} \left(\frac{m^2}{s} \right)$$

SI Unit : m2/s

For water at 20°C:

$$\nu = \frac{1.002 \times 10^{-3}}{1000} = 1.002 \times 10^{-6} \left(\frac{m^2}{s}\right)$$

The kinematic viscosity of fluids is particularly important in applications involving fluid flow in open channels, pipes, and the design of equipment like pumps.

1.2.7 Surface Tension (σ)

Surface Tension is the force that acts on the surface of a liquid per unit length, causing it to behave like a stretched elastic sheet. This property is responsible for phenomena like water droplets forming on surfaces and the ability of some insects to walk on water.

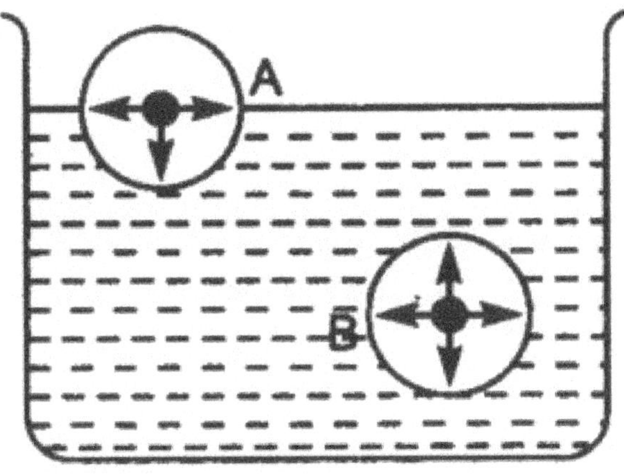

SI Unit : N/m

Surface tension depends on the liquid's nature and temperature. For example:

Water at 20°C: 0.072 N/m

Mercury at 20°C: 0.485 N/m

1.2.8 Capillarity

Capillarity is the ability of a liquid to rise or fall in a narrow tube without the assistance of external forces, due to the effects of surface tension. The height to which a liquid rises is influenced by the liquid's surface tension, the radius of the tube, and the density of the liquid.

Formula for capillary rise :

$$h = \frac{2\sigma\cos\theta}{\rho g r}$$

where:
h is the height the liquid rises,
σ (sigma) is the surface tension,
θ (theta) is the angle of contact,
ρ (rho) is the density of the liquid,
g is the acceleration due to gravity,
r is the radius of the tube.

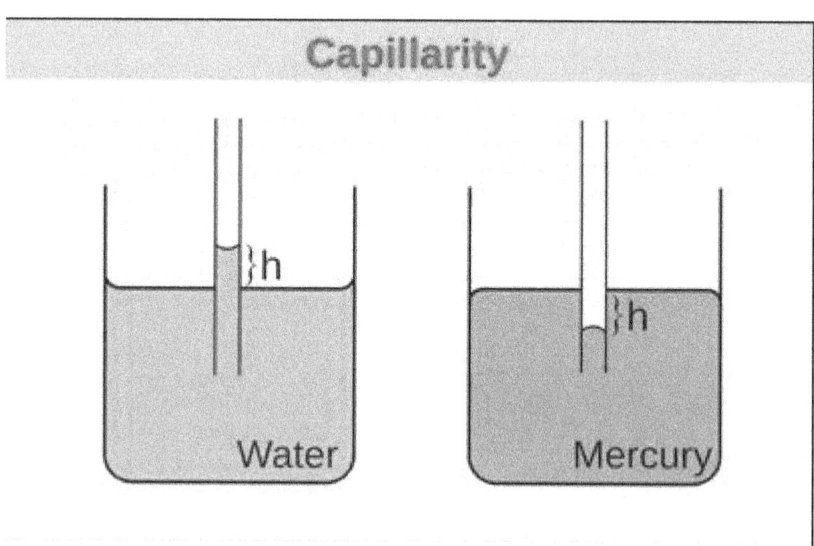

image shows capillarity ise and fall for different fluid

1.2.9 Vapour Pressure

Vapour Pressure is the pressure exerted by the vapor molecules when a liquid and its vapor are in equilibrium. It increases with temperature and is responsible for phenomena like evaporation and boiling.

For example:

Water at 20°C: 2.34 kPa

Ethanol at 20°C: 5.95 kPa

1.2.10 Compressibility (β)

Compressibility is the measure of a fluid's change in volume when subjected to pressure. Gases are much more compressible than liquids, and compressibility is particularly important in applications like gas pipelines, air conditioning, and weather forecasting.

Symbol for compressibility: β

Compressibility is inversely related to the bulk modulus K, where:

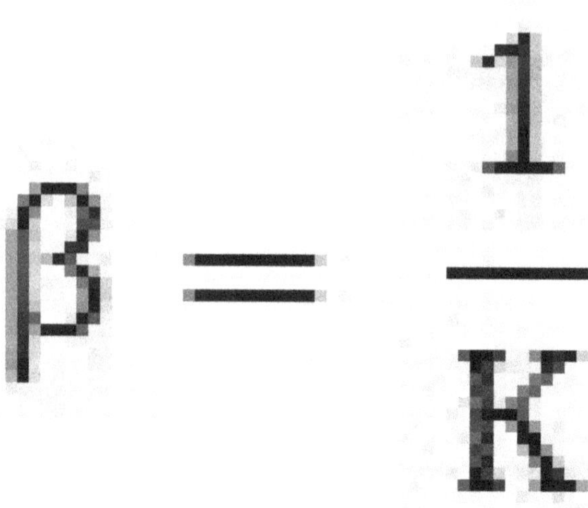

$$\beta = \frac{1}{K}$$

1.3 Types of Fluids

Fluids can be classified into different types based on their physical behavior and response to external forces like pressure and shear. Here is a simple explanation of different types of fluids with examples.

1.3.1 Ideal Fluid

Definition: A fluid that is incompressible (constant density) and has no viscosity (no internal resistance to flow). It is an imaginary concept used for theoretical analysis.

Example: No real-life example. It is an idealization used in fluid mechanics problems.

1.3.2 Real Fluid

Definition: A fluid that has viscosity and compressibility, and offers resistance to flow.

Example: Water, air, oil — all real fluids.

1.3.3 Newtonian Fluid

Definition: A fluid that follows Newton's law of viscosity, meaning the shear stress is directly proportional to the rate of shear strain.

Example: Water, air, kerosene.

1.3.4 Non-Newtonian Fluid

Definition: A fluid that does not follow Newton's law of viscosity. Its viscosity changes with the rate of shear strain.

Example: Toothpaste, blood, paint, ketchup.

1.3.5 Ideal Plastic Fluid

Definition: A fluid that behaves as a solid until a certain yield stress is applied, and then flows like a fluid.

Example: Bingham plastic materials like mud or toothpaste.

1.3.6 Compressible Fluid

Definition: A fluid whose density changes significantly when pressure or temperature changes.

Example: Air, steam, other gases.

1.3.7 Incompressible Fluid

Definition: A fluid whose density remains nearly constant even with pressure changes.

Example: Water (in most practical conditions), oil.

1.4 Newton's Law of Viscosity

Newton's Law of Viscosity states that the shear stress between adjacent layers of a fluid is directly proportional to the rate of change of velocity with respect to the distance between the layers. In simple words, when a fluid flows, its different layers move at different speeds, and the fluid resists this motion due to internal friction, which is called viscosity. According to Newton, this resistance or shear stress (denoted by τ) is proportional to the velocity gradient (du/dy), where 'u' is the velocity and 'y' is the distance between the fluid layers. The constant of proportionality is called dynamic viscosity (μ), and the formula is written as $\tau = \mu(du/dy)$. This law is applicable only to Newtonian fluids, in which viscosity remains constant at a given temperature. For example, fluids like water, air, and light oils follow Newton's law. In contrast, fluids like honey or paint may not obey this law under all conditions. Newton's law helps us understand how easily or how difficult it is for a fluid to flow when a force is applied.

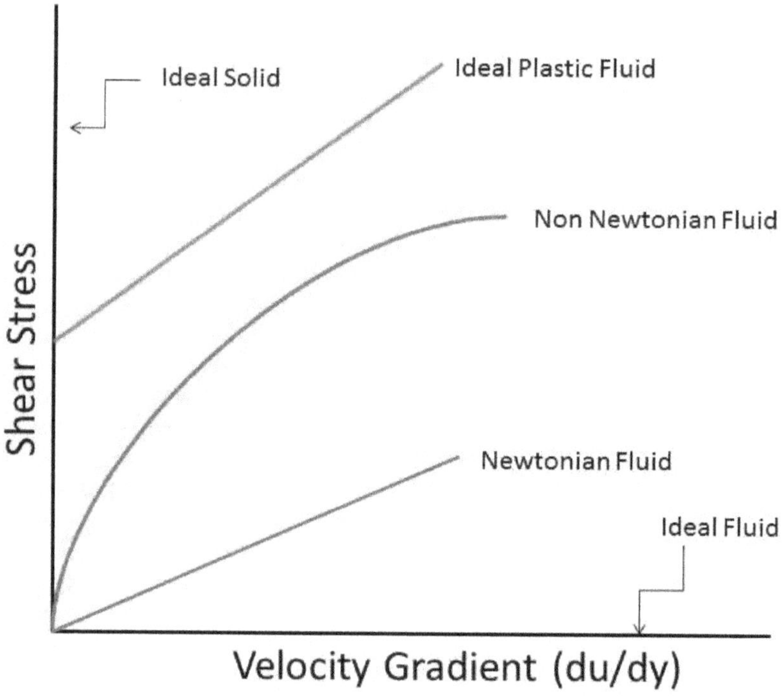

Figure shows relation between Shear stress and velocity gradient for different fluids

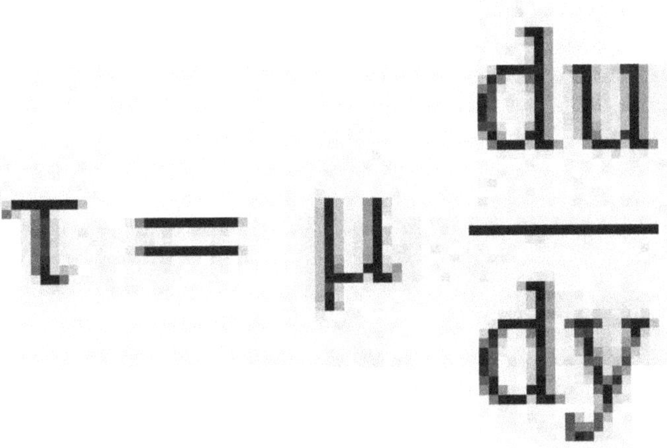

$$\tau = \mu \frac{du}{dy}$$

Where:

τ = Shear stress (N/m² or Pa)

μ = Dynamic viscosity of the fluid (Pa·s)

du/dy = Velocity gradient or rate of shear strain

1.5 Fluid Pressure

1.5.1 Fluid Pressure

Fluid Pressure is the force per unit area exerted by a fluid on the surface it comes in contact with. This pressure results from the molecular motion of the fluid particles, and it acts equally in all directions at a given point in a fluid (in static conditions).

The formula for pressure is:

$$P = \frac{Force}{Area} \left(\frac{m^2}{s}\right)$$

Pressure in Liquids and Gases

In liquids, pressure increases with depth, as the weight of the liquid above increases. In gases, pressure depends on the temperature, volume, and amount of gas present (described by the ideal gas law).

Example:

Consider a tank filled with water. At a depth h, the pressure at that point due to the water column above is given by:

P=ρ·g·h

Where:

ρ is the density of the fluid,

g is the acceleration due to gravity (9.81 m/s²),

h is the height of the fluid column.

For example, if you have a water tank with a height of 10 meters, the pressure at the bottom is:

P=1000 kg/m3 × 9.81 m/s2 × 10 m=98,100 Pa (or 98.1 kPa)

This illustrates how pressure increases with depth.

1.5.2 Pressure Head

Pressure Head is a measure of the height of a fluid column that corresponds to a given pressure. It is often used in fluid mechanics to simplify calculations when dealing with pressure in fluid flow problems. The pressure head can be calculated from the pressure using the following equation:

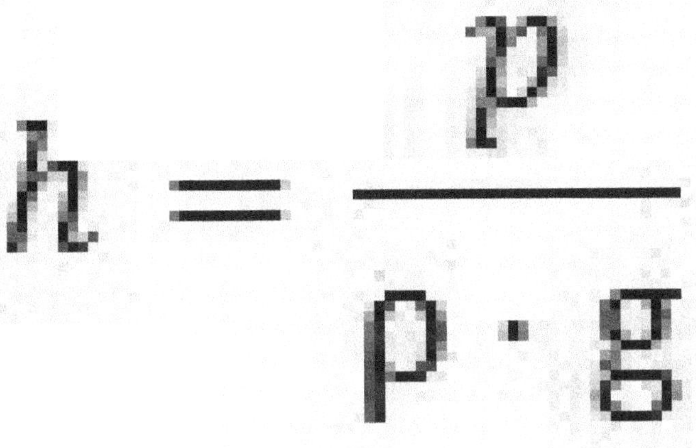

$$h = \frac{P}{\rho \cdot g}$$

Where:

h is the pressure head,

P is the pressure at the point of interest,

ρ is the density of the fluid,

g is the acceleration due to gravity.

Example:

If the pressure in a tank is 98,100 Pa, the corresponding pressure head for water would be:

$$h = \frac{98100}{1000 \cdot 9.81} = 10 \; meter$$

This indicates that the pressure is equivalent to the pressure exerted by a 10-meter column of water.

1.5.3 Types of Pressure

1.5.3.1 Atmospheric Pressure

Atmospheric Pressureis the pressure exerted by the Earth's atmosphere at any given point. It decreases with altitude. At sea level, the atmospheric pressure is approximately 101.3 kPa (or 1 atmosphere).

Atmospheric pressure is a crucial reference point in fluid mechanics because many measurement devices, like manometers, are calibrated to measure pressure relative to the atmospheric pressure.

1.5.3.2 Gauge Pressure

Gauge Pressure is the pressure measured relative to atmospheric pressure. If a pressure gauge reads 0, it means the pressure in the system is equal to the atmospheric pressure. If the pressure is higher than the atmospheric pressure, it will be positive; if lower, it will be negative.

$$Pgauge = Pabsolute - Patm$$

Example:

If a car tire has a gauge pressure of 200 kPa, the absolute pressure inside the tire is:

$$Pabsolute = Pgauge + Patm = 200 \, kPa + 101.3 \, kPa = 301.3 \, kPa$$

1.5.3.3 Absolute Pressure

Absolute Pressure is the total pressure exerted by a fluid, including atmospheric pressure. It is always positive, as it includes both the gauge pressure and the atmospheric pressure.

$$Pabsolute = Pgauge + Patm$$

Absolute pressure is important in applications where accurate pressure measurements are needed, such as in high-pressure steam boilers, gas pipelines, and vacuum systems.

1.5.3.4 Vacuum Pressure

Vacuum Pressure is the pressure below atmospheric pressure. It is expressed as a negative value (e.g., -50 kPa) and indicates the difference between the atmospheric pressure and the pressure in the system. Vacuum pressure is commonly used in systems that create a low-pressure environment, like vacuums in food storage or industrial processes.

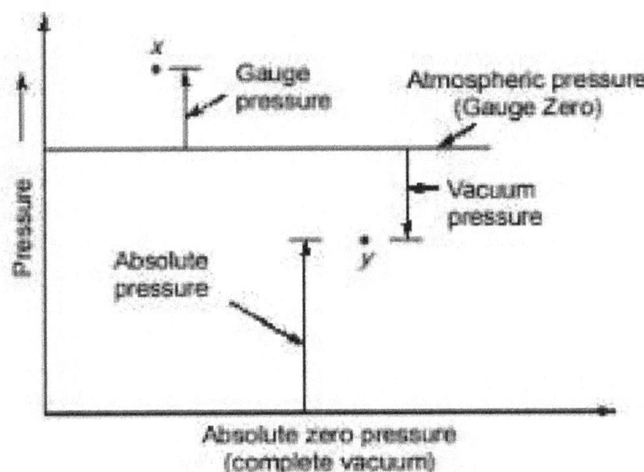

Relation Between different pressure

1.5.3 Pascal's Law

Pascal's Law is a fundamental principle in fluid mechanics that explains how pressure is transmitted in a fluid. Pascal's Law states that "When pressure is applied to a confined fluid, the increase in pressure is transmitted equally and undiminished in all directions throughout the fluid."

If you apply pressure at one point in a closed container filled with fluid (like water or oil), that pressure spreads equally in all directions. Every part of the fluid, and the walls of the container, will feel the same increase in pressure.

Example:

A hydraulic jack used to lift cars works on Pascal's Law. When a small force is applied to a small piston, it creates pressure in the oil, which is transmitted equally and pushes up a larger piston, lifting the car with a much larger force.

1.6 Pressure Measurement

1.6.1 Classification of pressure measurement device

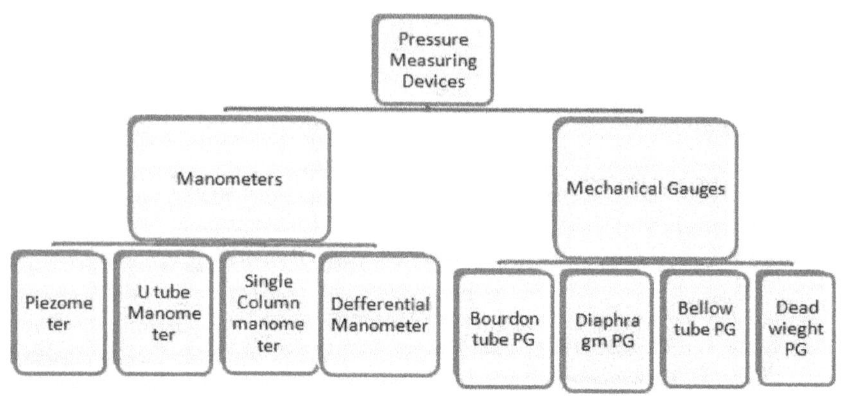

Types of Pressure Measuring Devices

1.6.2 Manometers – Explanation and Working

1.6.2.1 Piezometer

A vertical transparent tube connected to a pipe or tank at one end and open to the atmosphere at the other. When connected to a fluid system, the liquid rises in the tube to a height proportional to the pressure at that point. The height of the liquid column (h) gives the pressure head.

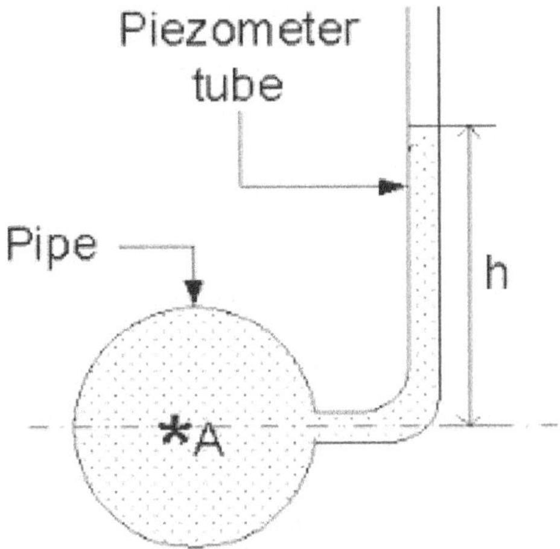

Piezometer Tube

$$P = \rho \cdot g \cdot h$$

Where:
ρ is Density of the liquid,
g Acceleration due to gravity,
h Height of the liquid column.

Limitations: Cannot be used for gases or negative pressure (vacuum), and unsuitable for high pressures.

1.6.2.2 Simple U-tube Manometer

A glass tube bent in a "U" shape. One end is connected to the pressure source, and the other may be open to the atmosphere or connected to another pressure source. The tube is partially filled with a manometric fluid (commonly mercury or water). When pressure is applied at one end, the fluid level in both arms changes. The difference in height (h) represents the pressure difference.

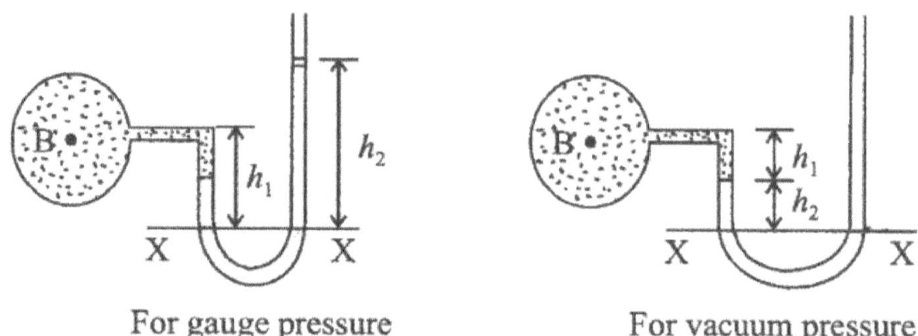

For gauge pressure   For vacuum pressure

Simple U tube manometer

Formula

$$P_B + \rho_B \cdot g \cdot h_1 = \rho_m \cdot g \cdot h_2$$

Case 1

$$P_B + \rho_B \cdot g \cdot h_1 - \rho_m \cdot g \cdot h_2 = 0$$

Case 2

Where P represents Pipe's pressure.

1.6.2.3 Single Column Manometer

A Single column manometer with reservoir is a type of pressure measuring device used to measure the pressure of a fluid, especially gases. It consists of a vertical tube connected to a large-diameter reservoir filled with a manometric fluid (usually mercury, water, or oil). It has two main parts: 1)Vertical glass tube (narrow) 2)Reservoir (wide) at the bottom. The reservoir is connected to a pipe or container whose pressure is to be measured. The vertical tube is open to the atmosphere (for gauge pressure measurement).

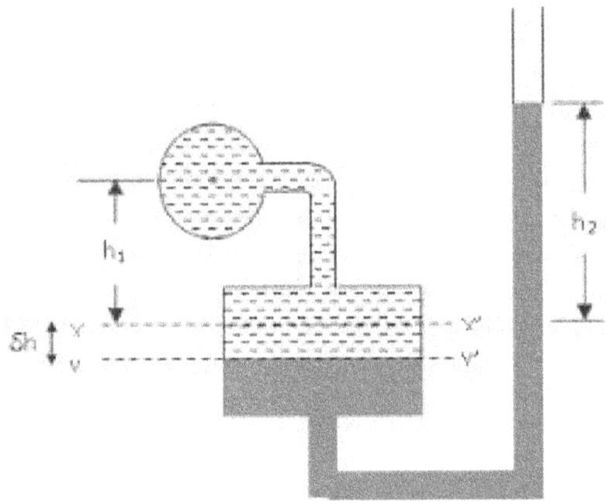

Single column Manometer

It works based on the hydrostatic pressure principle. When pressure is applied through the inlet connected to the reservoir: The fluid level in the reservoir goes down, and The fluid level in the vertical tube goes up. The pressure is measured by the difference in height (h) of the fluid column in the tube.Because the reservoir has a large cross-sectional area compared to the tube, the fluid level in the reservoir drops very little, and this drop can often be neglected in calculations.

1.6.2.4 Differential U tube manometer

A U-tube with both ends facing upward and filled with a light fluid (e.g., oil). Air or another light fluid may occupy the central part. Used when the pressure difference is small and the fluid being measured has higher density than manometric fluid.

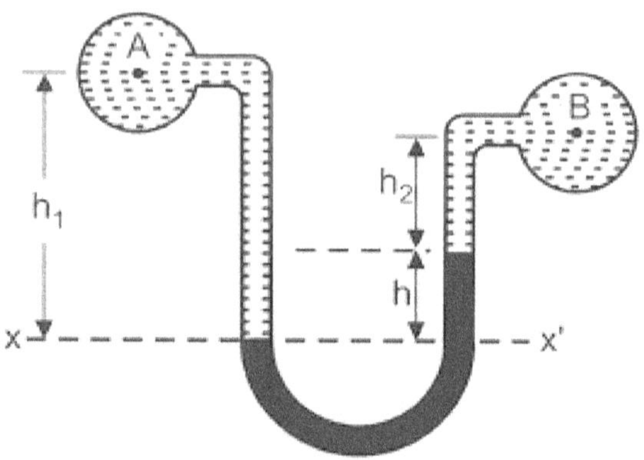

Differential U tube manometer

It measures pressure difference, not absolute or gauge pressure. Suitable for low-pressure applications. Very accurate and simple in design. No moving parts, so maintenance is minimal. Measuring pressure drop across valves, filters, or pipes. Used in fluid mechanics labs and industrial setups.

1.6.3 Mechanical gauges

1.6.3.1 Bourdon tube Perssure Gauge

A Bourdon tube pressure gauge is a mechanical device used to measure the pressure of gases or liquids. It is one of the most commonly used pressure measuring instruments in industries due to its simplicity, accuracy, and durability. In its construction the main part is a curved, hollow metal tube (called the Bourdon tube) shaped like a "C". One end of the tube is fixed and connected to the pressure inlet.The other end is free to move and is connected to a mechanical linkage and pointer.The entire assembly is enclosed in a circular dial casing.

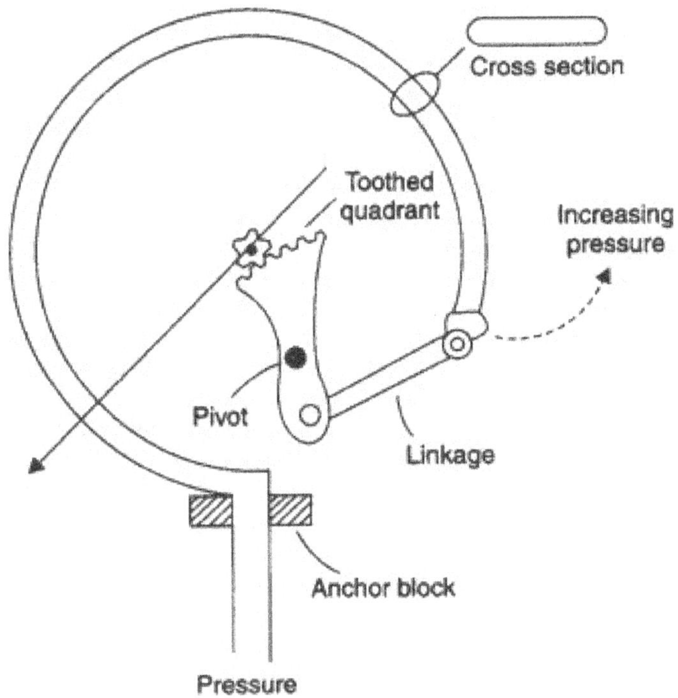

Bourdon tube pressure gauge

When pressure is applied inside the Bourdon tube, the cross-section tends to become circular, causing the tube to straighten slightly. This movement is transferred through mechanical linkages to a pointer that moves over a calibrated scale. The pointer indicates the pressure directly on the dial. The working is based on the principle that a curved tube tends to straighten when internal pressure increases.

Types of Bourdon Tubes:

C-type (most common, semi-circular)

Spiral-type

Helical-type

These types allow for different pressure ranges and sensitivities.

1.6.3.2 Diaphragm pressure gauge

A diaphragm pressure gauge is a type of mechanical pressure measuring instrument that uses a flexible diaphragm to sense pressure. It is especially useful for measuring low pressures and for corrosive or viscous fluids where other gauges might not work well. The main component is a thin, elastic metal diaphragm (circular in shape). The diaphragm is clamped between two flanges to form a sealed chamber. One side of the diaphragm is exposed to the pressure to be measured. The diaphragm is connected to a mechanical linkage and pointer, which shows the pressure on a calibrated dial.

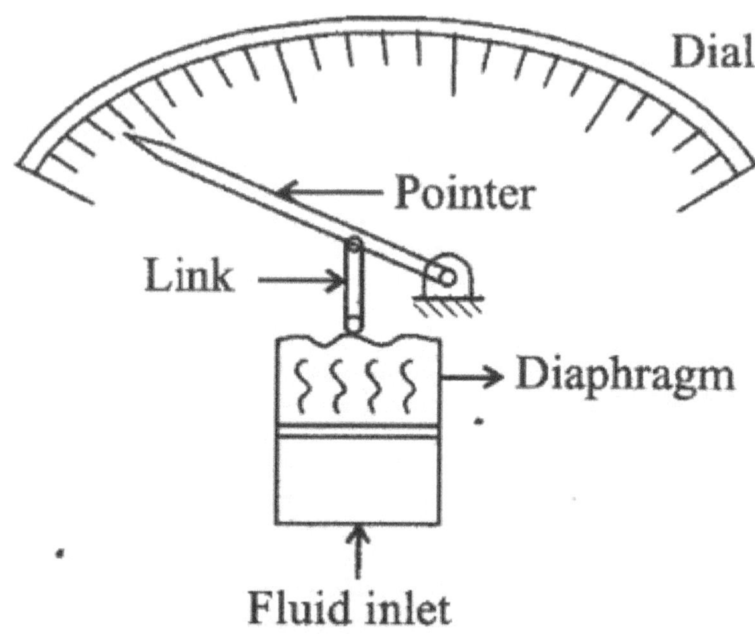

Diphragm Pressure Gauge

When pressure is applied to one side of the diaphragm,The diaphragm deflects (bends) in response to the pressure. This deflection is proportional to the pressure applied. The movement of the diaphragm is transmitted through a mechanical linkage to a pointer, which indicates the pressure on the dial. The basic principle is: The diaphragm deflects when pressure is applied, and this movement is used to measure the pressure.

Types of Diaphragm Gauges:

Single-diaphragm (for general use)

Capsule type (two diaphragms joined together – for very low pressures)

1.6.3.3 Bellow tube pressue gauge

A bellow tube pressure gauge is a mechanical instrument used to measure low to moderate pressures. It works by using a thin-walled, collapsible metal bellow that expands or contracts when pressure is applied. The main part is a bellows: a flexible, accordion-like metallic tube. One end of the bellows is fixed, while the other end is free to move. The bellows is connected to a mechanical linkage and a pointer. The entire assembly is housed inside a casing with a calibrated dial.

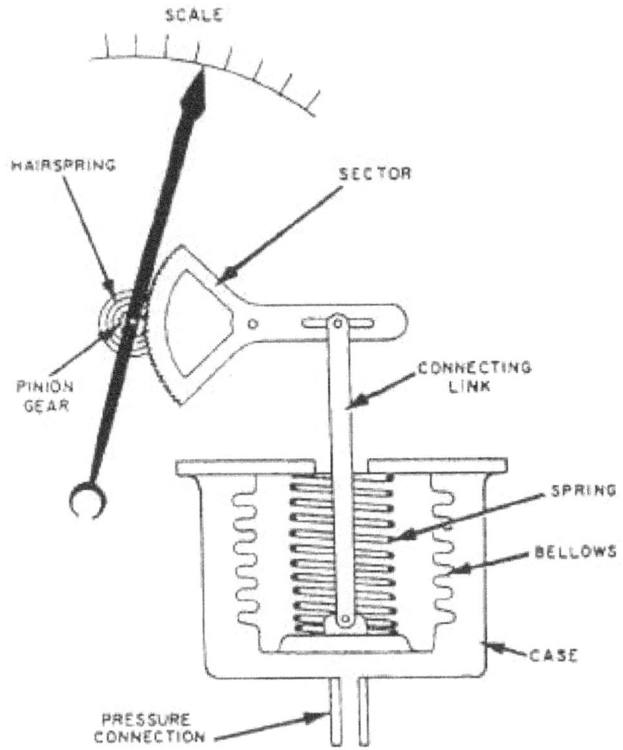

Bellow tube pressure gauge

When pressure is applied inside the bellows, The bellows expand or contract depending on the amount of pressure. This linear movement is transmitted to a pointer through a gear and linkage mechanism. The pointer moves over a dial, indicating the pressure value. The gauge works on the principle that bellows expand or compress when pressure changes, and this movement is used to indicate pressure.

Types of Pressure Measured:

Gauge pressure

Vacuum pressure

Differential pressure (with double bellows)

1.6.3.4 Dead weight pressure gauge

A dead weight pressure gauge (also called a dead weight tester) is a highly accurate pressure-measuring device used mainly for calibrating other pressure gauges. It works based on a very basic and reliable principle: pressure = force / area. It consists of a cylinder and piston assembly. A set of known standard weights is provided. The piston is connected to a pressure chamber, which is also connected to the gauge to be tested. A fluid (usually oil) is used to transmit pressure. There is a spindle or rotating knob to spin the weights and reduce friction.

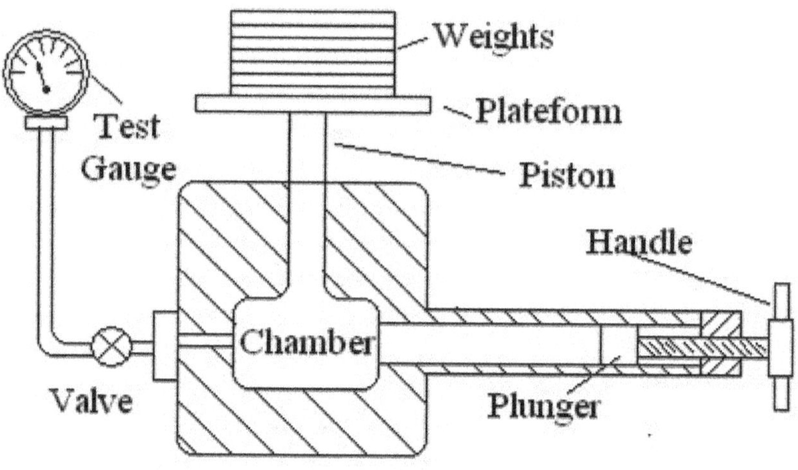

Dea weight pressure gauge

The fluid is pumped until the piston starts rising. Standard weights are placed on top of the piston. The piston moves up and down slightly, indicating equilibrium. The pressure gauge connected to the system shows the pressure value, which should match the pressure calculated from the weights.

Simple Numericals

Q: A U-tube manometer is connected to a pipe carrying water. One limb is open to atmosphere and the other connected to the pipe. The difference in mercury levels is 0.15 m. Determine the gauge pressure at the pipe section.

Solution:

Given:

h=0.15 m of Hg

ρ(Hg) = 13,600 kg/m3

ρ(water) = 1000 kg/m3

g = 9.81 m/s2

$$p = \rho_{Hg} \cdot g \cdot h = 13{,}600 \cdot 9.81 \cdot 0.15 \approx 20000 \text{ Pa}$$

Or in meters of water column:

$$h_{water} = 0.15 \times \frac{13{,}600}{1000} = 2.04 \text{ m}$$

Answer: Gauge pressure = 20,000 Pa or 2.04 m of water

CHAPTER TWO

FLUID FLOW AND FLOW THROUGH PIPES

2.1 Fluid flow

Fluid flow refers to the movement of a fluid (liquid or gas) from one place to another, typically due to a difference in pressure or elevation. It is an important concept in fluid mechanics and is governed by various principles.

2.1.1 Important terms

2.1.1.1 Stream line

A streamline is a line that represents the path followed by fluid particles in a flow field at a particular instant. It is a useful concept in fluid mechanics for visualizing the direction and behavior of fluid flow. At every point along a streamline, the tangent to the line indicates the direction of the fluid velocity at that point. In other words, if a small particle were placed in the fluid, it would move along the streamline.

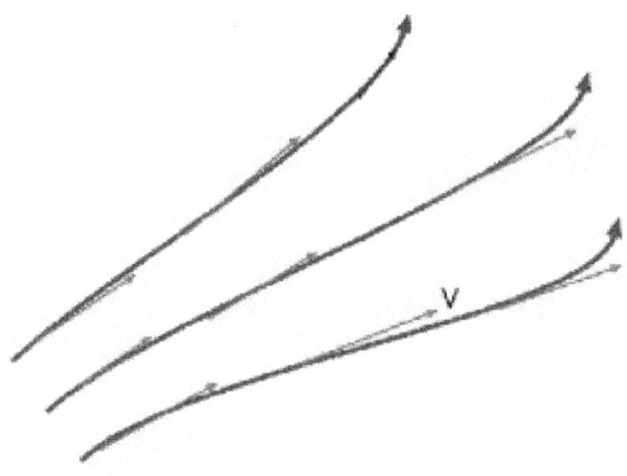

Stream line

2.1.1.2 Path line

A path line is the actual trajectory or path that a single fluid particle follows as it moves through a flow field over time. Unlike a streamline, which represents the direction of flow at a specific instant, a path line shows the history of a fluid particle's motion. To visualize a path line, imagine injecting a small, visible dye particle into a flowing fluid and tracking its movement; the trail left behind is the path line.

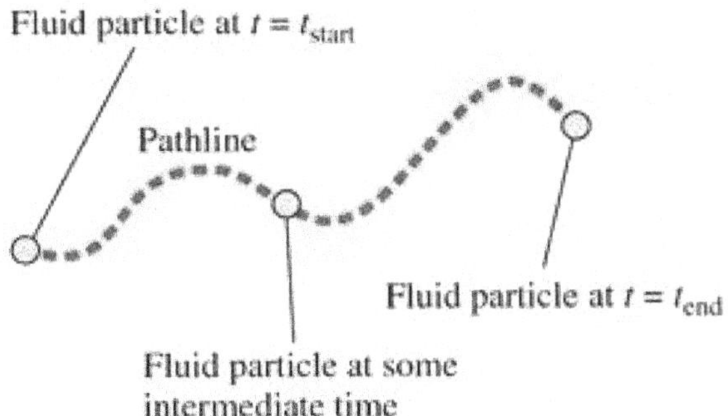

Path line

2.1.1.3 Streak line

A streak line is a line that represents the loci of fluid particles that have passed through a particular point in the flow field over a certain period of time. Unlike streamlines and path lines, which deal with the behavior of a single particle at a given instant (streamline) or the trajectory of a single particle over time (path line), a streak line traces the continuous set of fluid particles that have passed through the same point.

2.1.1.4 stream tube

A streamtube is a conceptual volume of fluid bounded by streamlines in a flow field. It can be thought of as a "tube" formed by adjacent streamlines, within which the flow remains steady and continuous. The fluid entering and exiting a streamtube does so without any leakage across the boundaries, as the streamlines define the boundaries of the flow.

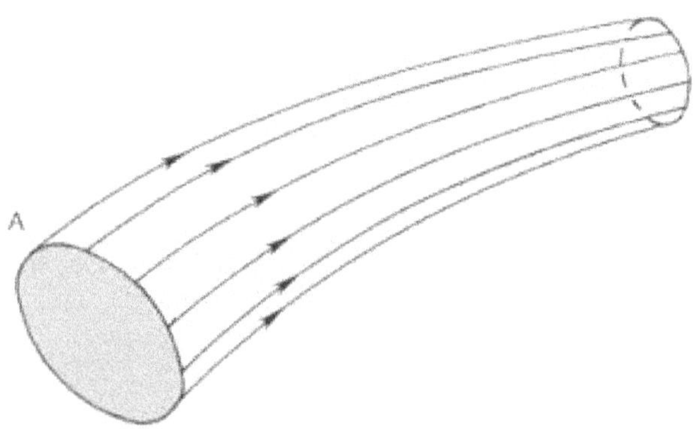

Stream tube

2.1.2 Types of flow

2.1.2.1 steady flow and unsteady flow

Steady Flow

In steady flow, the fluid's velocity at any given point does not change with time. This means that if you were to measure the velocity of the fluid at a specific point at different times, it would always be the same. The properties of the fluid, such as pressure, density, and velocity, remain constant at any particular point in the flow field.

Unsteady flow

In unsteady flow, the velocity of the fluid at any given point changes over time. This means that the flow conditions, such as velocity, pressure, and density, can vary from moment to moment at any specific location in the flow field. Unsteady flow is typically seen in many real-world applications, where factors like turbulence, changes in flow rate, and varying external conditions cause the flow to fluctuate over time.

2.1.2.2 Uniform flow and Non-Uniform flow

Uniform Flow

In uniform flow, the velocity of the fluid at every point along a specific direction (such as along a pipe or stream) remains constant. This means that the speed and direction of the fluid particles do not change as you move along the flow path. The flow is uniform in the sense that it doesn't vary with position, either in the spatial or temporal domain.

Non-Uniform Flow

In non-uniform flow, the velocity of the fluid changes from one point to another along the flow direction. This means that the speed and direction of the fluid particles vary as you move through the flow field. Non-uniform flow can be caused by factors like changes in pipe diameter, bends in the flow path, or varying flow rates.

2.1.2.3 Rotational flow and Irrotational flow

Rotational Flow

In rotational flow, the fluid particles exhibit rotational motion, meaning that at any given point in the flow, the fluid particles have some degree of angular velocity or vorticity. Essentially, fluid particles rotate around their own axis as they move through the flow field.

Irrotational Flow

In irrotational flow, the fluid particles do not have any rotational motion. This means that the fluid particles move in such a way that their rotation (or vorticity) is zero. The flow is smooth and uniform without any swirling or spinning behavior in the fluid.

2.1.2.4 Compressible flow and Incompressible flow

Compressible Flow

In compressible flow, the fluid density changes significantly due to variations in pressure and temperature. This is typically observed in gases or in situations where the fluid moves at high speeds, such as in the case of supersonic or high-speed flows. In compressible flow, the volume of the fluid can vary substantially as the fluid passes through different parts of the system.

Incompressible Flow

In incompressible flo.w, the fluid density remains nearly constant throughout the flow, even if there are changes in pressure or temperature. This simplification is typically valid for liquids because their density doesn't change significantly under most conditions. In incompressible flow, the fluid behaves as if its volume is fixed, which greatly simplifies the analysis of the flow

2.1.2.5 Laminar flow and Turbulent flow

Laminar Flow:

In laminar flow, the fluid moves in smooth, parallel layers or "laminae." The flow is orderly, with minimal mixing between the layers of fluid. In this type of flow, the fluid particles move in a regular, predictable manner, and the velocity of the fluid varies only slightly across different layers.

Turbulent Flow:

In turbulent flow, the fluid moves chaotically, with irregular fluctuations and eddies (swirling motion). The flow is characterized by random and chaotic variations in velocity, pressure, and direction. Turbulent flow involves a high degree of mixing between the fluid layers, resulting in complex flow patterns.

2.1.2.6 One dimensional flow, Two dimensional flow and Three dimensional flow

One-Dimensional Flow:

In one-dimensional flow, the fluid properties (like velocity, pressure, and density) vary only along one spatial direction—usually along the length of the flow path. Variations in the other two directions (width and height) are assumed negligible.

Two-Dimensional Flow:

In two-dimensional flow, fluid properties vary in two spatial directions but remain constant in the third direction. This means the flow characteristics change in a plane (e.g., x and y directions), but not in the perpendicular direction (z).

Three-Dimensional Flow:

In three-dimensional flow, the fluid properties vary in all three spatial directions (x, y, and z). This represents the most realistic and complex type of flow.

2.1.3 Discharge or Flow rate (Q)

Discharge (Q) refers to the volume of fluid flowing per unit time through a cross-section of a pipe, channel, or any flow area. It is a key concept in fluid mechanics and hydraulics, used to measure how much fluid passes a certain point in a given time.

$$Q = A \times V \text{ (SI unit } m^3/s)$$

Where:

Q = Discharge (volume flow rate)

A = Cross-sectional area of the flow (in m2)

V = Average velocity of the fluid (in m/s)

Example:

If water flows through a pipe with a cross-sectional area of 0.5 m^2 at a velocity of 2 m/s, then:

$$Q = A \times V = 0.5 \times 2 = 1 \, m^3/s$$

2.1.4 Conttinuity Equation

The continuity equation is a fundamental principle in fluid mechanics based on the conservation of mass. It states that mass cannot be created or destroyed within a flow system.

For incompressible, steady flow, the volume flow rate (discharge) remains constant throughout the flow.

For steady, incompressible flow:

$$\text{Mass flow rate at section 1} = \text{Mass flow rate at section 2}$$

$$\rho A1 V1 = \rho A2 V2$$

Where ρ is the density of fluid (constant for incompressible fluid). Cancel ρ from both sides:

$$A1 V1 = A2 V2$$

This is the continuity equation for incompressible flow. If the pipe becomes narrower (i.e., A2 < A1), then to maintain the same flow rate, the velocity must increase (V2 > V1).

2.1.5 Bernoulli's Equation

Bernoulli's Equation is a principle of energy conservation in fluid dynamics. It states that for a steady, incompressible, and frictionless flow, the total mechanical energy per unit weight of fluid remains constant along a streamline.

Assumptions in berrnoulli's equation

Steady flow

Incompressible fluid

No friction (ideal flow)

Flow along a streamline

$$\frac{dP}{\rho} + V\,dV + g\,dz = 0$$

From Euler's equation for frictionless flow

$$\frac{P}{\rho} + \frac{V^2}{2} + gz = \text{constant}$$

Integrating between two points gives

$$\frac{P}{\rho g} + \frac{V^2}{2g} + z = \text{constant}$$

Divide the entire equation by g to convert it to head terms

Bernoulli's equation shows that if the fluid velocity increases, the pressure or potential energy must decrease, and vice versa. It's a powerful tool for analyzing fluid flow in pipes, nozzles, or open channels.

2.2 Flow measuring Devices

2.2.1 Classification of flow measuring devices

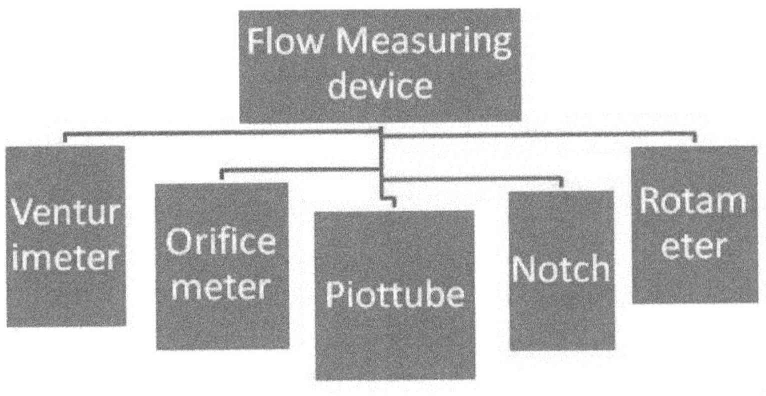

Flow meauring devices

2.2.2 Venturimeter

A Venturimeter is a device used to measure the flow rate (discharge) of a fluid flowing through a pipeline. It works on the principle of conversion of pressure energy into kinetic energy as described by Bernoulli's equation.

Parts of a Venturimeter:

Converging Section : This is the first part of the Venturimeter, where the pipe gradually narrows. The fluid enters this section from the main pipeline. As the cross-sectional area decreases, the velocity of the fluid increases, and pressure drops (according to Bernoulli's equation). The smooth taper (usually at 20° to 22° angle) prevents flow separation and minimizes energy loss.

Throat : This is the middle, narrowest section of the Venturimeter. Because of the smallest cross-sectional area, the fluid reaches its maximum velocity here. As per Bernoulli's principle, this results in the lowest pressure in the throat. A differential manometer is often connected between the inlet and throat to measure the pressure drop.

Diverging Section : This is the outlet section, where the pipe widens gradually (usually with a 5° to 7° angle). As the area increases, the velocity decreases, and pressure increases again. The gradual expansion is designed to recover pressure and reduce energy loss due to turbulence.

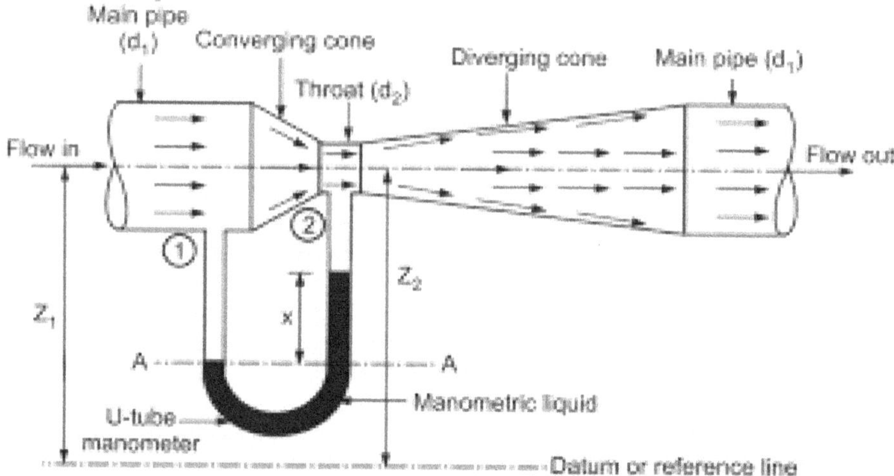

Venturimeter

Working Principle of Venturimeter:
Fluid enters the converging section, its velocity increases and pressure drops. At the throat, velocity is maximum, and pressure is minimum. A manometer (U-tube or differential) measures the pressure difference between the inlet and throat. This pressure difference is then used to calculate discharge (Q) using Bernoulli's and continuity equations.

$$Q = C_d \cdot A_2 \cdot \sqrt{\frac{2gh}{1 - \frac{A_2}{A_1}^2}}$$

Q = Discharge (m³/s)
Cd = Coefficient of discharge (typically between 0.96–0.98)
A1 = Area of inlet (m²)

A2 = Area of throat (m^2)

g = Acceleration due to gravity (9.81 m/s^2)

h = Pressure head difference (in meters of fluid column)

Applications of Venturimeter :

- Measuring water flow in pipes and irrigation systems
- Monitoring flow in chemical and oil pipelines
- Fuel flow measurement in engines
- Industrial and hydraulic testing setups

2.2.3 Orifice meter

An Orifice Meter is a simple and cost-effective device used to measure the rate of flow (discharge) of a fluid through a pipe. It consists of a thin plate with a sharp-edged hole (called an orifice) mounted inside a pipeline. The flow measurement is based on Bernoulli's principle and the resulting pressure drop across the orifice.

Main Parts of an Orifice Meter (With Detailed Function):

Orifice Plate : A flat metal plate with a circular hole (orifice) at its center. It is inserted perpendicular to the fluid flow in the pipe. The sharp-edged hole causes a sudden reduction in flow area, increasing velocity and decreasing pressure.

Inlet and Outlet Sections : These are the portions of the pipe before and after the orifice plate. The inlet pressure (before the orifice) is higher than the outlet pressure (after the orifice).

Pressure Taps (or Pressure Points) : Two pressure taps are located, One before the orifice plate (upstream) One after the orifice plate (downstream). These taps are connected to a differential manometer to measure the pressure drop.

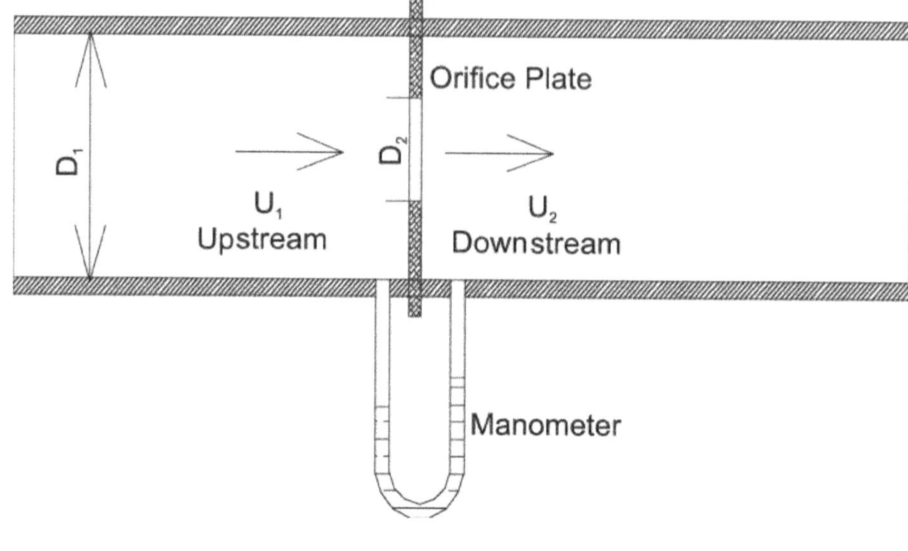

Orifice meter

Working Principle of an Orifice Meter :
Fluid flows through the pipe and reaches the orifice plate. As it passes through the narrow orifice, its velocity increases and pressure decreases. The pressure difference between the upstream and downstream sides is measured. This pressure drop is used to calculate the discharge using Bernoulli's equation combined with the continuity equation.

$$Q = C_d \cdot A_2 \cdot \sqrt{\dfrac{2gh}{1 - \dfrac{A_2}{A_1}^2}}$$

Q = Discharge (m³/s)
Cd = Coefficient of discharge (typically between 0.6–0.65)
A1 = Area of inlet (m²)
A2 = Area of throat (m²)
g = Acceleration due to gravity (9.81 m/s²)
h = Pressure head difference (in meters of fluid column)

Applications of Orfice Meter :

- Water and gas flow measurement
- Steam flow measurement in power plants
- Oil and fuel flow monitoring
- Temporary or economical flow measurement installations

2.2.4 Pitot tube

Pitot Tube is a simple device used to measure the velocity of a fluid flowing through a pipe or in open air (such as wind). It works based on the principle of conversion between kinetic energy and pressure energy, as described by Bernoulli's equation.

It is widely used in aerodynamics, hydraulics, and fluid mechanics to measure the local velocity at a particular point in the flow stream.

Main Parts of a Pitot Tube:

Impact Tube (Forward-facing tube) : A small tube facing directly into the flow. It measures total (stagnation) pressure — the pressure when fluid velocity becomes zero at the stagnation point.

Static Tube (Side-facing holes) : Holes provided on the side of the tube or on a separate tube mounted in the same region. Measures static pressure of the fluid.

Manometer or Pressure Sensor : Connected to the impact and static tubes. Measures the difference between total pressure and static pressure, known as dynamic pressure.

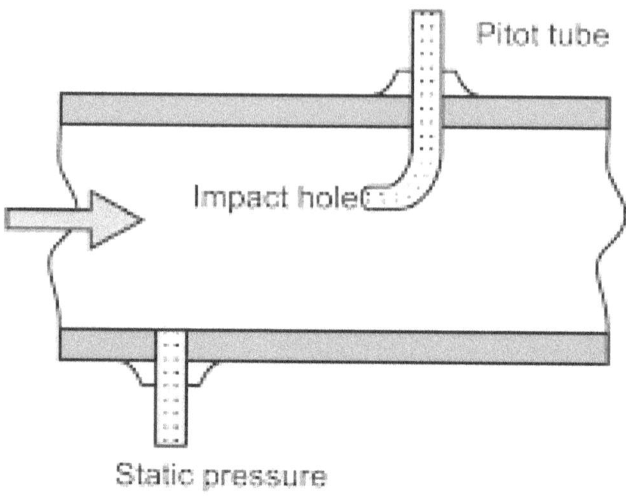

Pitot tube

Working Principle of Pitot Tube:

When fluid enters the forward-facing tube, it is brought to rest (stagnation), and the stagnation pressure is recorded. The side holes sense the static pressure of the fluid. The difference between stagnation pressure and static pressure gives the dynamic pressure, which is used to calculate velocity using Bernoulli's equation.

$$V = C \cdot \sqrt{2gh}$$

V = Fluid velocity (m/s)
C = Correction factor (usually ≈ 0.98–1.0)
g = Acceleration due to gravity (9.81 m/s²)
h = Difference in manometer reading (pressure head, in meters)

Applications of Pitot Tube:

- Measuring airspeed in aircraft
- Determining velocity profiles in rivers, pipelines, or wind tunnels
- Testing ventilation systems and HVAC flows
- Calibration of flow meters

2.2.5 Notch

A Notch is a specially shaped opening or cut-out in a tank or channel wall, typically used to measure the discharge (flow rate) of a liquid. It allows water to flow over the edge in a controlled manner, and the height of the liquid (head) above the bottom of the notch is used to calculate the discharge.

Notches are generally used in open channel flow measurements, such as in labs, irrigation canals, and small dams.

Working Principle of a Notch:

The liquid flows over the notch under the action of gravity.

As it passes through the notch, it accelerates and forms a free jet.

The height of liquid (H) above the notch sill determines the velocity and discharge.

Bernoulli's equation and integration over the notch profile give the discharge formula.

Types of Notches:

Rectangular Notch: A notch with a rectangular opening.

Can be: Sharp-crested (thin plate), Broad-crested.

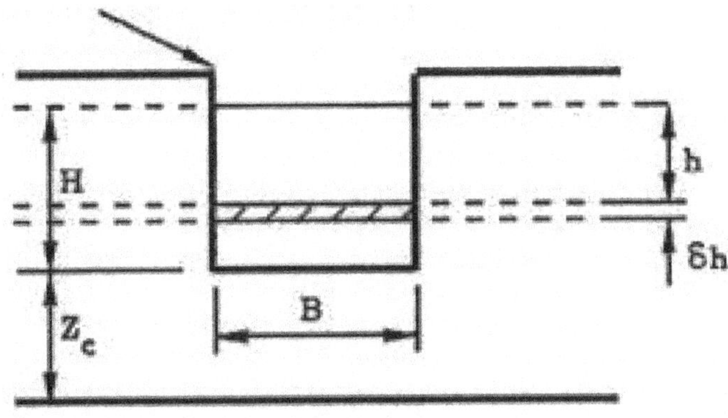

Rectangular Notch

$$Q = \frac{2}{3}C_d \cdot b \cdot \sqrt{2g} \cdot H^{3/2}$$

b = width of notch (m)
H = head of water above sill (m)
Cd = coefficient of discharge ($\approx$ 0.6–0.65)

Triangular or V-Notch:
A notch in the shape of a 'V' (usually 90° or 60° angle). More accurate at low flow rates.

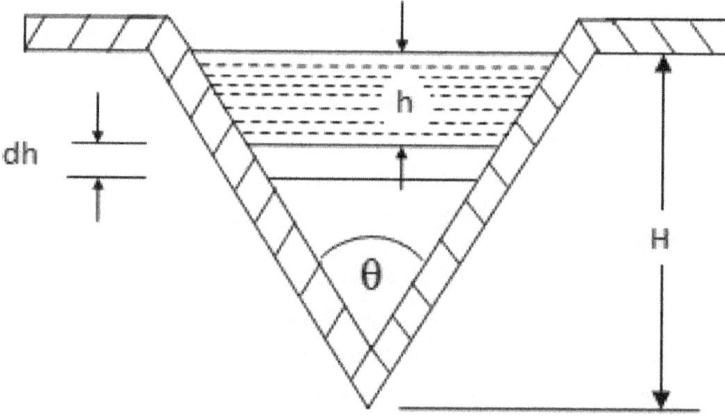

V Notch

$$Q = \frac{8}{15} C_d \cdot \tan\frac{\theta}{2} \cdot \sqrt{2g} \cdot H^{5/2}$$

θ = angle of notch
H = head over notch

Trapezoidal Notch (Cipolletti Notch):
A combination of rectangular and triangular notches. Side slopes are generally 1 horizontal to 4 vertical.
More accurate than rectangular notch.

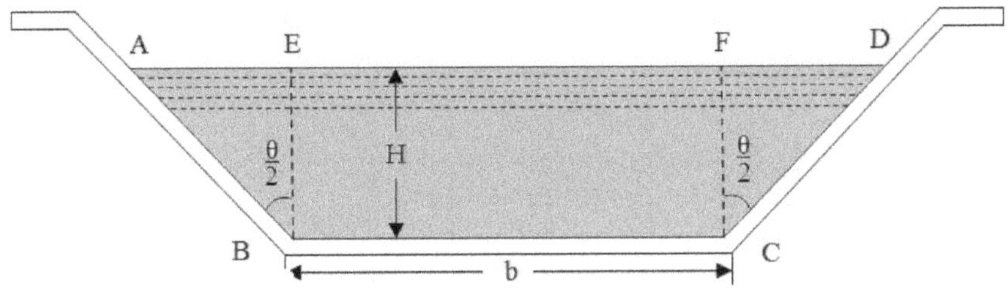

Trapezoidal Notch

$$Q = \frac{2}{3} C_d \cdot b \cdot \sqrt{2g} \cdot H^{3/2} + \frac{8}{15} C_d \cdot \tan\frac{\theta}{2} \cdot \sqrt{2g} \cdot H^{5/2}$$

2.2.6 Rotameter

A Rotameter is a variable area flow meter used to measure the flow rate of liquids or gases in a closed tube. It consists of a vertically oriented tapered tube with a float inside, which rises or falls depending on the flow rate. It operates based on the balance between the upward fluid force and the downward gravitational force acting on the float.

Main Parts of a Rotameter:

Tapered Transparent Tube : Usually made of glass or plastic. Widens from bottom to top, allowing the float to rise with increasing flow.

Float : A weighted object (often stainless steel or plastic) inside the tube. Floats freely up or down depending on the flow rate.

Scale/Graduation : Marked on the tube or nearby panel. Indicates the flow rate corresponding to the float's position.

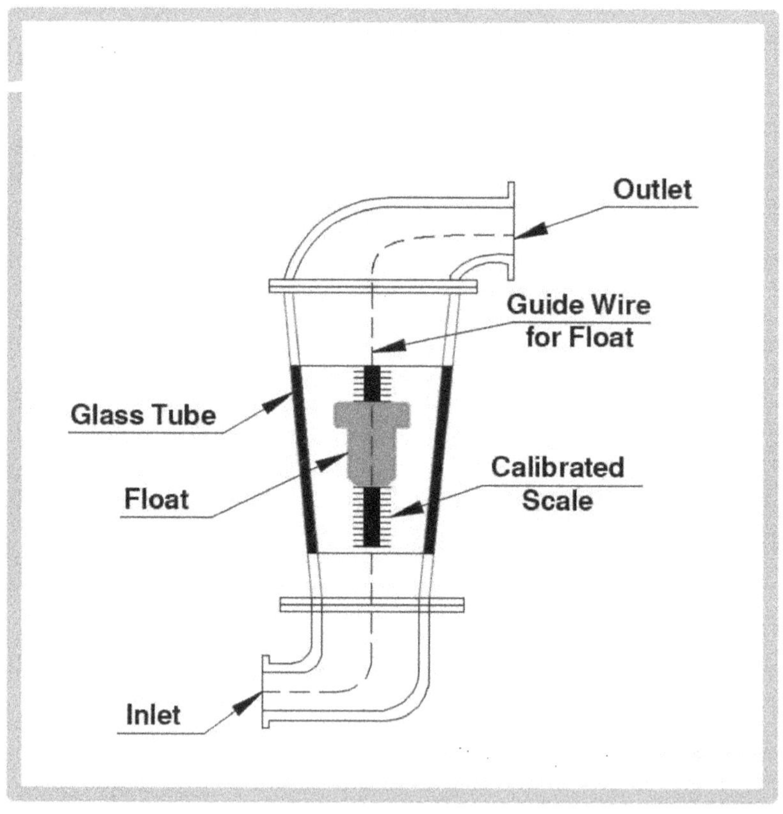

Rotameter

Working Principle of a Rotameter:

Fluid enters the bottom of the tapered tube and flows upward. The float is lifted by the fluid velocity and suspended at a point where the upward drag force equals the downward weight of the float. The higher the flow rate, the higher the float rises, since a larger area is needed to balance the flow. The position of the float is directly proportional to the flow rate.

2.3 Flow Through Pipes

Flow through pipes refers to the movement of fluids (usually liquids) through a closed conduit or pipe. This flow is governed by principles of fluid mechanics and is affected by various factors like pressure, velocity, pipe diameter, and friction.

2.3.1 Raynold's experiment

Reynolds' experiment is a fundamental fluid mechanics demonstration conducted by Osborne Reynolds in the 19th century to study the nature of fluid flow in a pipe. The experiment was designed to visualize and distinguish between laminar, transitional, and turbulent flow. It also introduced the concept of the Reynolds number, a dimensionless quantity used to predict the flow regime based on fluid properties and flow conditions.

The experimental setup consists of a transparent horizontal glass tube connected to a tank of water. A small nozzle is used to introduce a thin stream of colored dye (such as ink) into the center of the flow. The flow rate of water is controlled using a valve at the outlet, allowing the observer to vary the speed of the fluid inside the tube. As the fluid flows through the tube, the behavior of the dye streak provides a visual representation of how the fluid moves.

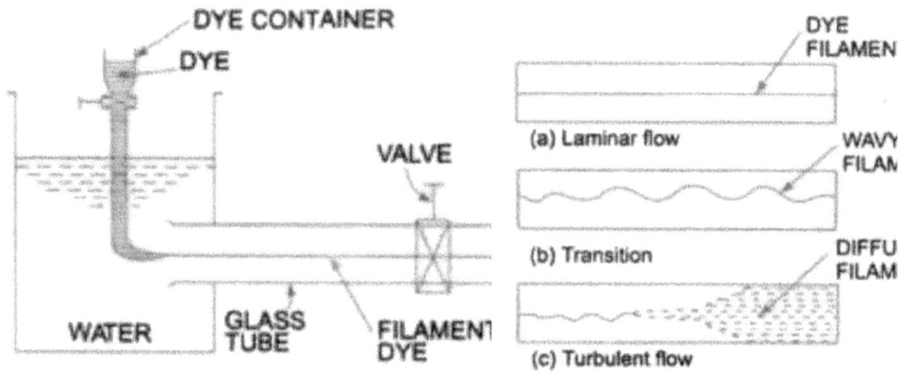

Raynold's Experiment

At low velocities, the dye travels in a straight, smooth line, indicating laminar flow, where fluid particles move in parallel layers with minimal mixing. As the velocity increases, the dye begins to fluctuate and wiggle, indicating the transitional flow region, which is unstable and may switch between laminar and turbulent. At high velocities, the dye disperses randomly throughout the tube, showing turbulent flow, where the fluid particles move in a chaotic and irregular manner.

Reynolds derived a mathematical expression to determine the type of flow, now known as the Reynolds Number (Re) :

$$Re = \frac{\rho v D}{\mu} = \frac{v D}{\nu}$$

Re = Reynolds number
ρ = density of fluid (kg/m³)
v = average velocity of flow (m/s)
D = diameter of pipe (m)

μ = dynamic viscosity (Pa·s)

v = kinematic viscosity (m²/s)

Based on the Reynolds number, the nature of flow can be categorized as:

Laminar Flow : Re < 2000

Transitional Flow : 2000 < Re < 4000

Turbulent Flow : Re > 4000

This experiment is crucial for engineers and scientists as it helps in understanding how fluids behave in different systems like pipelines, blood vessels, and hydraulic circuits. It also plays a key role in the design of flow meters, pumps, and other fluid handling equipment.

2.3.2 Darcy's equation and Chezy's equation

Darcy's Equation

Darcy's Equation, also known as the Darcy-Weisbach equation, is used to calculate the head loss (energy loss) due to friction in a pipe during fluid flow. This loss depends on factors such as the pipe length, diameter, flow velocity, and friction factor. It is applicable for both laminar and turbulent flow, but the friction factor differs for each case. The formula is :

$$h_f = \frac{f \cdot L \cdot v^2}{2g \cdot D}$$

hf = head loss due to friction (m)

f = Darcy friction factor (dimensionless)

L = length of pipe (m)

D = diameter of pipe (m)

v = flow velocity (m/s)

g = acceleration due to gravity (9.81 m/s²)

This equation is important in pipe design, water supply systems, and industrial piping to ensure that pressure loss remains within acceptable limits.

Chezy's Equation

Chezy's Equation is used to determine the average velocity of flow in open channels like canals, rivers, and partially filled pipes. It relates the flow velocity to the hydraulic radius and slope of the channel, with the help of the Chezy constant (C), which depends on the surface roughness and flow conditions. The equation is :

$$v = C\sqrt{R \cdot S}$$

v = average velocity of flow (m/s)
C = Chezy's constant (m½/s), depends on roughness and flow type
R = hydraulic radius (m) = A/P
S = slope of the channel (head loss per unit length)

Chezy's equation is particularly useful for analyzing and designing open channel flow systems, including irrigation channels, stormwater drains, and sewer lines.

2.3.3 Water hammer effect

The Water Hammer Effect is a hydraulic phenomenon that occurs when a flowing fluid is suddenly forced to stop or change direction in a pipeline. This sudden change causes a pressure surge or wave to travel through the pipe, which can result in loud banging noises and even damage to the pipe or fittings. It is commonly observed in long pipelines or when valves are closed quickly.

When water is flowing in a pipe and a valve is shut abruptly, the momentum of the moving water creates a high-pressure shock wave that travels back through the fluid. Since liquids are nearly incompressible, the kinetic energy of the flowing fluid is suddenly converted into pressure energy. This rapid increase in pressure can stress the pipe walls, burst joints, or damage valves and pumps.

Reasons for Water Hammer Effect

The water hammer effect occurs primarily due to the sudden stoppage or rapid change in fluid flow within a pipeline. This can happen when a valve is closed quickly, a pump is turned off suddenly, or fluid flow is interrupted by a mechanical failure. Since fluids are incompressible, the abrupt momentum change causes a pressure surge or shock wave to travel back through the system. The longer and faster the flow in the pipe, the more severe the water hammer.

Prevention Methods for Water Hammer

Slow Valve Operation: Use slow-closing valves to allow gradual changes in flow, reducing sudden pressure build-up.

Air Chambers or Surge Tanks: Install air chambers or surge tanks to absorb the shock waves and reduce pressure spikes.

Pressure Relief Valves: These valves automatically release excess pressure when it builds up due to water hammer.

Pipe Anchoring and Supports: Properly support and anchor the pipes to reduce vibrations and mechanical stress.

Use of Check Valves: Install non-slam check valves that prevent reverse flow and sudden stoppage in fluid movement.

Gradual Pump Start/Stop: Use variable speed drives or soft starters for pumps to avoid abrupt changes in flow velocity.

2.4 Minor losses in pipes

In fluid flow through pipes, energy is lost due to friction and flow disturbances. These losses are categorized into major losses (due to friction along the pipe length) and minor losses, which occur at pipe fittings, bends, valves, and other flow interruptions. Despite being called "minor," these losses can be significant in systems with many fittings or short pipe lengths.

Losses due to Sudden Enlargement

When fluid moves from a smaller to a larger diameter pipe, it slows down suddenly, causing eddies and pressure loss.

$$h_e = \frac{\left(v_1 - v_2\right)^2}{2g}$$

Where v1 and v2 are velocities before and after enlargement.

Losses due to Sudden Contraction

Flow entering a smaller pipe forms a vena contracta, leading to turbulence and energy loss.

$$h_c = K_c \cdot \frac{v^2}{2g}$$

Typical Kc ≈ 0.5

Losses due to Bends and Elbows
Changes in flow direction cause separation and swirling, leading to pressure loss.

$$h_b = K_b \cdot \frac{v^2}{2g}$$

Typical Kb ≈ 0.2–0.9 depending on angle and radius

Valves (Gate, Globe, Ball)
Valves restrict and control flow; partially open valves cause significant losses.

$$h_v = K_v \cdot \frac{v^2}{2g}$$

Typical Kv :
Gate valve (fully open) : ≈ 0.2
Globe valve (open) : ≈ 10

T-Junctions or Y-Junctions
Splitting or combining flows in pipelines causes additional turbulence.

$$h_j = K_j \cdot \frac{v^2}{2g}$$

Kj depends on flow direction and angle.

2.5 Hydraulic Gradient line and Total Gradient line

Hydraulic Gradient Line (HGL)

The Hydraulic Gradient Line represents the variation of pressure head plus datum head (elevation) along the length of a pipe. It shows the height to which water would rise in piezometer tubes connected to the pipe. Mathematically, it is given by :

$$HGL = \frac{p}{\gamma} + z$$

p/γ = pressure head (m)z = elevation head (m)

In a flowing pipeline, if the flow is open to atmosphere (like in an open channel), the HGL coincides with the free surface. In a pressurized pipe, it lies below or above the pipe depending on pressure (positive or negative).

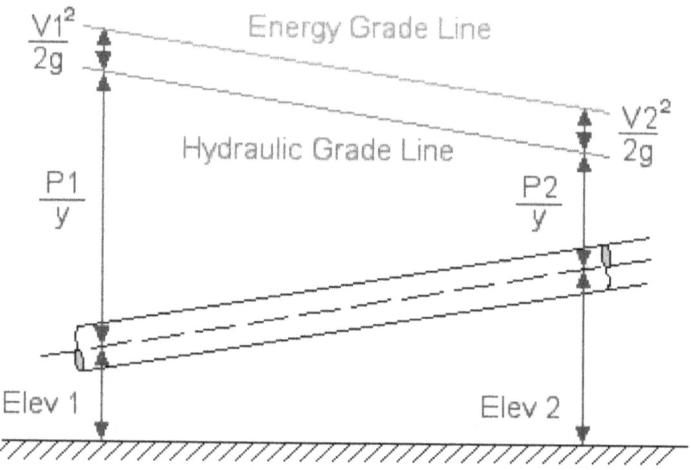

Total Energy Line (TEL or TGL)

The Total Energy Line represents the total mechanical energy of the fluid per unit weight, including pressure head, elevation head, and velocity head. It indicates the total energy available at any cross-section in the flow. It is given by :

$$\text{TEL} = \frac{p}{\gamma} + z + \frac{v^2}{2g}$$

v2 / 2g = velocity head (m)

Since velocity is always positive in flow, the TEL always lies above the HGL by the amount of velocity head. If the fluid is at rest (v = 0), both TEL and HGL coincide.

Simple Numericals

Q: Water flows through a 100 m long pipe of diameter 0.2 m at a velocity of 2 m/s. If the friction factor f=0.02, calculate the head loss due to friction.

Solution:
Given:
Length L = 100 m
Diameter D = 0.2 m
Velocity v = 2 m/s
Friction factor f = 0.02
g = 9.81 m/s²

$$h_f = \frac{f \cdot L \cdot v^2}{2g \cdot D}$$

Substitute values:

$$h_f = \frac{0.02 \times 100 \times 2^2}{2 \times 9.81 \times 0.2} = \frac{0.02 \times 100 \times 4}{3.924} = \frac{8}{3.924} \approx 2.038 \text{ m}$$

Answer: Head loss due to friction = 2.04 m

Q: A venturimeter is installed in a horizontal pipe carrying water. The inlet diameter is 0.2 m, throat diameter is 0.1 m, and the differential manometer shows a reading of 0.2 m of mercury. Calculate the discharge. Take Cd=0.98C_d = 0.98Cd=0.98.
Solution:
Given:
D1 = 0.2 m, D2 = 0.1 m
h=0.2 m of Hg
Cd=0.98
ρ(Hg) = 13,600 kg/m3
ρ(water) = 1000 kg/m3
g=9.81 m/s2
Convert pressure head:

$$h_{water} = 0.2 \times \frac{13,600}{1000} = 2.72 \text{ m}$$

Area:

$$A_1 = \frac{\pi}{4}D_1^2 = 0.0314 \text{ m}^2, \quad A_2 = \frac{\pi}{4}D_2^2 = 0.00785 \text{ m}^2$$

$$Q = C_d A_2 \sqrt{\frac{2gh}{1 - (A_2/A_1)^2}}$$

$$Q = 0.98 \times 0.00785 \times \sqrt{\frac{2 \times 9.81 \times 2.72}{1 - (0.00785/0.0314)^2}}$$

$$Q \approx 0.0077 \times \sqrt{\frac{53.38}{1 - 0.0625}} = 0.0077 \times \sqrt{56.98} = 0.0077 \times 7.55 \approx 0.0582 \text{ m}^3/s$$

Discharge = 0.0582 m³/s

CHAPTER THREE

IMPACT OF JETS

3.1 Introduction

The impact of jet is a fundamental concept in fluid mechanics, especially in the field of hydraulic machinery. It involves the study of the force exerted by a fluid jet when it strikes a surface. This surface can be stationary or moving, flat or curved. Understanding how jets apply force is essential in the design and analysis of turbines, nozzles, vanes, and many other hydraulic machines.

Basic Concept

A jet is a stream of fluid (usually water in hydraulic machines) emerging from an orifice or nozzle with high velocity. When this jet strikes a surface, it transfers momentum to the surface, creating a force. This is based on Newton's Second Law of Motion, which states :

Force = Rate of change of momentum

In fluid terms:

$$F = \frac{d(mv)}{dt} = \rho AV(V - V_s)$$

F = Force exerted by the jet

ρ = Density of fluid (kg/m³)

A = Cross-sectional area of jet (m²)

V = Velocity of the jet (m/s)

Vs = Velocity of the surface struck (m/s)

3.2 Impact of Jet on a Stationary Vertical Plate

Introduction

When a high-speed jet of fluid (usually water) strikes a surface, it exerts a force due to the change in momentum. One of the simplest and most fundamental cases is when a jet of water strikes a stationary vertical plate perpendicularly. Understanding this scenario is essential as it forms the basis for studying more complex interactions like those in turbines and jet propulsion systems.

Physical Setup

A jet of fluid with velocity V and cross-sectional area A emerges from a nozzle and strikes a vertical flat plate. The plate is stationary and smooth, meaning it does not absorb the fluid nor does it offer resistance through friction. The fluid is assumed to be incompressible and the flow is steady (i.e., all parameters like velocity, pressure remain constant over time).

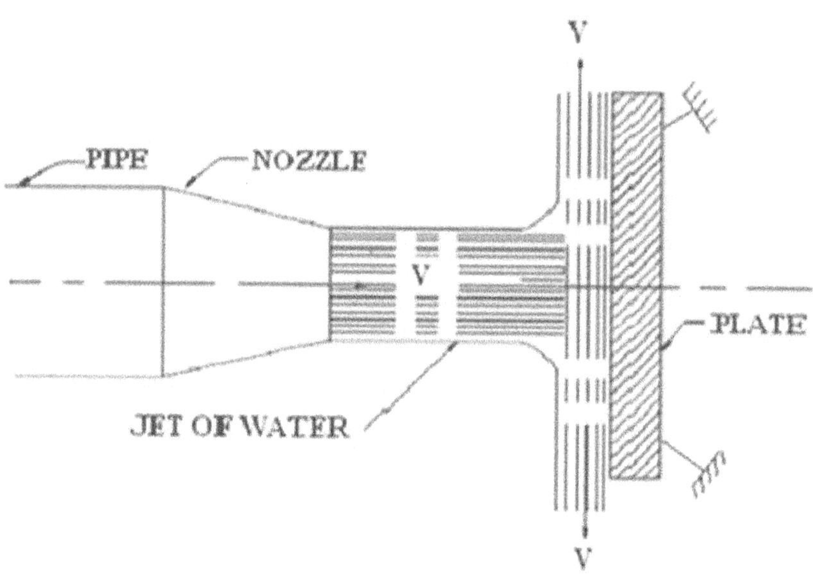

Impact of Jet on a Stationary Vertical Plate

Assumptions
The jet is uniform and has a constant velocity V.
The plate is large enough to completely stop the jet (no fluid escapes around it).
The plate does not deform under the impact.
No energy loss due to friction or turbulence (ideal case).
Explanation Using Momentum Principle
According to Newton's Second Law:
Force (F)=Rate of change of momentum
The mass flow rate of the fluid striking the plate is:

$$\dot{m} = \rho AV$$

Where:
ρ = Density of the fluid (kg/m³)
A = Area of jet (m²)
V = Velocity of jet (m/s)
Initially, the momentum of water in the direction of jet flow is :

$$\text{Initial Momentum} = \dot{m} \cdot V = \rho AV \cdot V = \rho AV^2$$

After hitting the plate, the fluid is deflected sideways (parallel to the plate), so the final velocity in the original direction becomes zero.

$$\text{Final Momentum} = 0$$

So, the change in momentum is:

$$\Delta p = \rho AV^2$$

Therefore, the force exerted by the jet on the plate is:

$$F = \rho A V^2$$

Direction of Force

The force acts perpendicular to the surface of the plate, in the direction opposite to the jet's motion. Since the plate is vertical and the jet strikes horizontally, the force is horizontal.

No Work Done

Work is defined as:

$$\text{Work Done} = \text{Force} \times \text{Displacement}$$

Since the plate is stationary, displacement = 0, so:

$$\text{Work Done} = 0$$

This implies that although the jet exerts a force, it does no mechanical work on the stationary plate.

Real-World Example

Imagine a firefighter holding a water hose. When the water jet hits a wall (a vertical surface), he feels a backward push. That is due to the impact force from the jet on the wall. In hydraulic systems, understanding this force helps in designing structures like deflectors and energy-dissipating plates.

3.3 Impact of Jet on a Moving Flat Plate

Introduction

When a jet of fluid strikes a plate that is moving in the same direction as the jet, the resulting force and energy transfer are different compared to the stationary plate case. This concept is crucial in the study of hydraulic turbines and jet propulsion, where moving vanes or blades interact with high-velocity fluid jets.

Physical Setup

A fluid jet with velocity V and cross-sectional area A strikes a flat plate moving in the direction of the jet with a constant velocity u. The jet strikes perpendicularly to the plate surface. The plate is smooth, and the fluid is assumed to flow without friction. The flow is steady, and the fluid is incompressible.

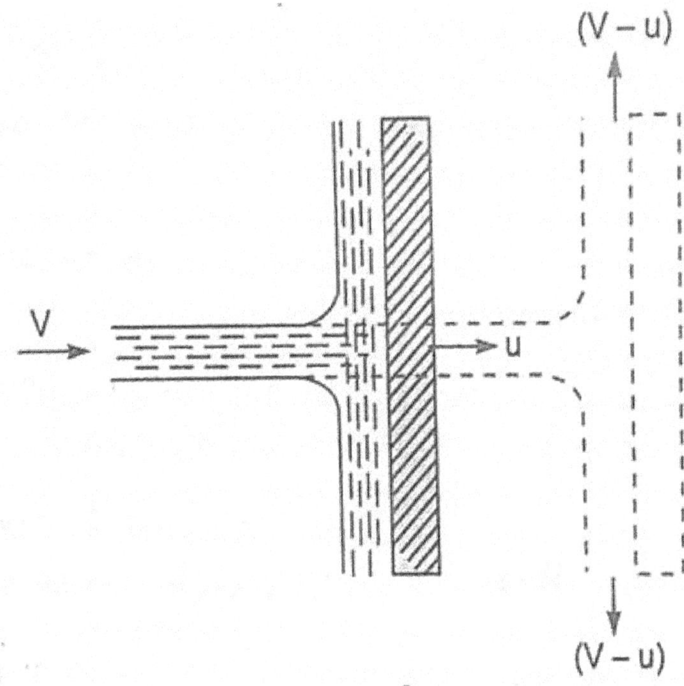

Impact of Jet on a Moving Flat Plate

Assumptions

The flow is steady and the jet has a constant velocity.

The plate moves in the same direction as the jet with velocity u, where u<V.

The plate surface is large enough to intercept the entire jet.

There is no loss of energy due to turbulence or friction (ideal conditions).

Velocity of Jet Relative to the Plate

From the plate's frame of reference, the jet appears to approach with a relative velocity of :

$$V_{rel} = V - u$$

After impact, the water sticks to the plate and moves with it (ideal case), so the final velocity of fluid relative to plate is zero.

Mass Flow Rate

The volume flow rate striking the plate = A(V−u)

So, mass flow rate of the fluid hitting the plate is:

$$\dot{m} = \rho A(V-u)$$

Change in Momentum

Initial momentum of fluid relative to ground = $\dot{m} \cdot V = \rho A(V-u) \cdot V$

Final momentum (after adhering to the plate) = $\dot{m} \cdot u = \rho A(V-u) \cdot u$

So, Change in momentum per second:

$$\Delta p = \rho A(V-u)(V-u-u) = \rho A(V-u)(V-2u)$$

According to Newton's second law:

F = Rate of change of momentum= $\rho A(V-u)(V-u-u) = \rho A(V-u)(V-2u)$

So, the force exerted by the jet on the moving plate is:

$$F = \rho A(V-u)(V-2u)$$

Work Done by the Jet

Work done is the force times the displacement of the plate:

$$\text{Work done per second} = F \cdot u = \rho A(V-u)(V-2u) \cdot u$$

This indicates the rate of energy transfer from the fluid jet to the moving plate.

Efficiency η is the useful work output divided by the kinetic energy input:

η=Work Done per second / Kinetic Energy supplied per second

Kinetic Energy supplied per second :

$$KE = \frac{1}{2}\rho A V^3$$

$$\eta = \frac{F \cdot u}{\frac{1}{2}\rho A V^3} = \frac{2u(V-u)(V-2u)}{V^3}$$

This is used to find the optimal velocity uuu for maximum efficiency, particularly in turbine design.

3.4 Impact of Jet on a Steady Inclined Plate

Introduction

When a jet of water strikes a stationary inclined plate, the jet's momentum is divided into two components: one perpendicular and one parallel to the surface of the plate. Analyzing the impact helps in understanding how forces are developed in hydraulic machines, especially in blades or vanes of turbines and deflectors.

Physical Setup

A fluid jet with velocity V and cross-sectional area A strikes a flat plate that is inclined at an angle θ with the direction of the jet. The plate is stationary. The plate is smooth, causing the jet to glide along the surface without friction. The fluid is assumed to be ideal (incompressible and no viscosity).

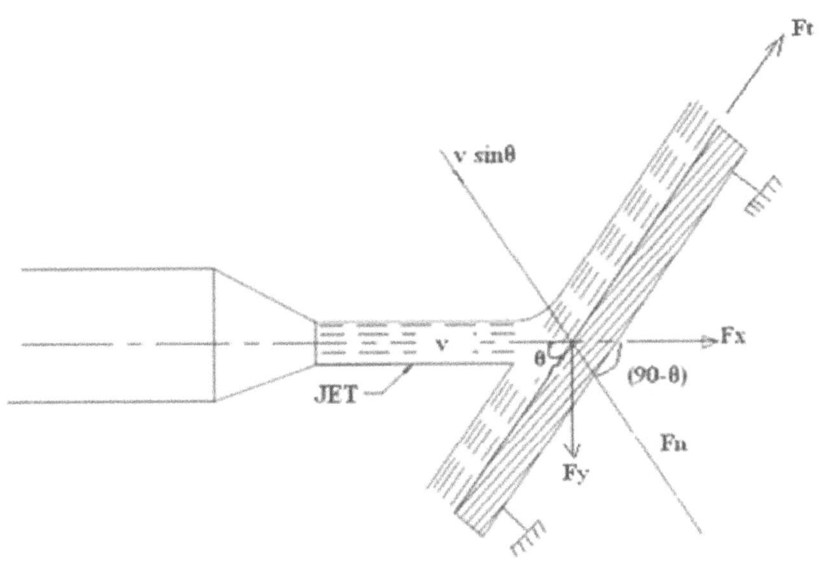

Assumptions

- The jet hits the plate normally and is deflected along the plane of the plate.
- The plate is fixed (no motion).
- The flow is steady and frictionless.
- The entire jet strikes the plate.
- The flow after striking is deflected and leaves the plate tangentially.

Velocity Components

The initial velocity of the fluid jet : V

The jet strikes the plate and slides along its surface, leaving at the same speed but in a different direction.

The component of velocity normal to the plate :

$$V_n = V \sin \theta$$

The component of velocity parallel to the plate:

$$V_t = V \cos \theta$$

After striking, the jet continues to move along the plate, meaning no velocity component remains normal to the plate (ideal deflection). Thus, only the normal component of momentum is altered.

Mass Flow Rate

The mass flow rate of the jet is:

$$\dot{m} = \rho A V$$

Force on the Plate

Only the normal component of the velocity causes a force on the plate, since the fluid slides along the surface after impact.

The change in momentum in the direction normal to the plate is:

$$\Delta p = \dot{m} \cdot V \sin\theta = \rho A V^2 \sin\theta$$

So, the force on the plate normal to its surface:

$$F_n = \rho A V^2 \sin^2\theta$$

To find the force in the direction of the jet (horizontal direction):

$$F_x = F_n \cdot \sin\theta = \rho A V^2 \sin^2\theta \cdot \sin\theta = \rho A V^2 \sin^3\theta$$

To find the force in the vertical direction (perpendicular to jet but along the plate):

$$F_y = F_n \cdot \cos\theta = \rho A V^2 \sin^2\theta \cdot \cos\theta$$

Final Velocity of Jet

Since the plate is frictionless, the jet slides along the inclined surface without loss of speed, exiting with the same velocity V, but direction changed.

3.5 Impact of jet on Moving inclined plate

Introduction

When a jet of fluid strikes a smooth inclined plate that is moving, the analysis involves resolving the velocities and forces in the direction of the plate's motion. This concept is useful in understanding momentum transfer in various fluid machinery components and is essential in the design of fluid handling systems.

Physical Setup

Let the velocity of the jet be V. Let the velocity of the inclined plate be uuu, in the same direction as the jet. The plate is inclined at an angle θ to the direction of the jet. The jet strikes the plate normally to its surface, and the fluid is assumed to glide smoothly over the plate without separation.

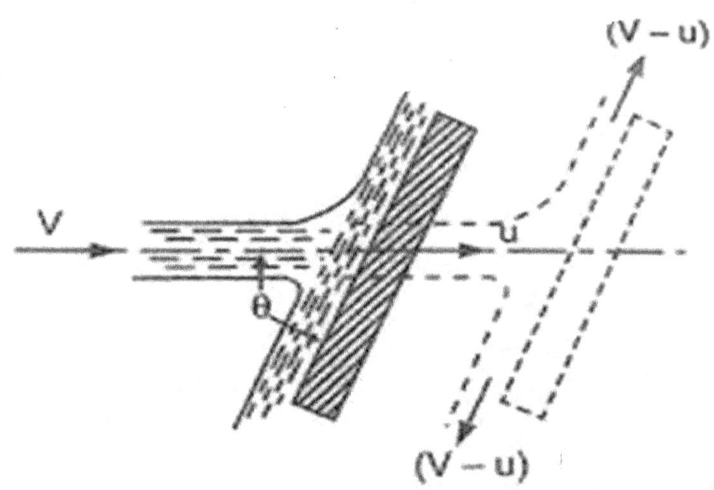

Assumptions

- The flow is steady, incompressible, and frictionless.
- The jet strikes the center of the plate and is deflected along the plate.
- The plate is smooth and thin, and it moves with uniform velocity.
- Relative velocity remains constant during impact due to frictionless assumption.

Relative Velocity

To analyze the momentum change, we consider the relative velocity between the jet and the plate:

Inlet relative velocity: V–u

The jet moves along the plate's surface after striking (no rebound or loss). Hence, outlet relative velocity is also V–u but in the inclined direction.

Force Exerted by Jet on the Plate

Let the area of the jet be A, and ρ be the density of the fluid.

Mass flow rate striking the plate:

$$\dot{m} = \rho A(V-u)$$

To calculate the force on the plate, we resolve velocities and forces in the direction of motion of the plate, i.e., in the horizontal direction.

Horizontal component of inlet velocity = (V−u)cos θ

Horizontal component of outlet velocity = (V−u)cos θ (same magnitude, same direction)

However, the fluid slides along the plate after impact, so we consider momentum change in the direction normal to the plate, which contributes to the effective force. But since the flow does not reverse, and assuming the jet glides along the plate, the net momentum in the plate's motion direction results in the reaction force :

$$F = \dot{m} \cdot (V - u) \cos^2 \theta$$

$$F = \rho A (V - u)^2 \cos^2 \theta$$

This is the force exerted by the jet on the inclined moving plate in the direction of motion.

Work Done by the Jet

Work done per second = Force × Velocity of plate =

$$W = F \cdot u = \rho A (V - u)^2 \cos^2 \theta \cdot u$$

This is the power transferred to the moving plate.

Efficiency of Jet Impact

Efficiency is the ratio of work done by the jet on the plate to the kinetic energy of the jet supplied per second :

$$\eta = \frac{W}{\frac{1}{2}\rho A V^3} = \frac{2u(V - u)^2 \cos^2 \theta}{V^3}$$

This efficiency is maximum when the plate velocity uuu is optimally matched to the jet velocity V, and the angle of inclination θ affects the effective momentum change.

3.6 Impact of Jet on a Steady Curved Plate

Introduction

When a jet of fluid strikes a curved plate that is stationary (steady), the direction of the fluid changes as it follows the curvature of the plate. This change in direction results in a greater force exerted on the plate as compared to a flat plate. Such a situation is commonly seen in Pelton wheel buckets and other hydraulic machines designed to extract energy from a fluid jet.

Physical Setup

A jet of water having velocity V, cross-sectional area A, and density ρ strikes a stationary curved plate.The curved plate is smooth and deflects the jet through an angle θ, measured from the initial jet direction to the final exit direction.The plate may be symmetric or asymmetric, and the jet may deflect either in the same plane or in three dimensions, depending on the curvature.

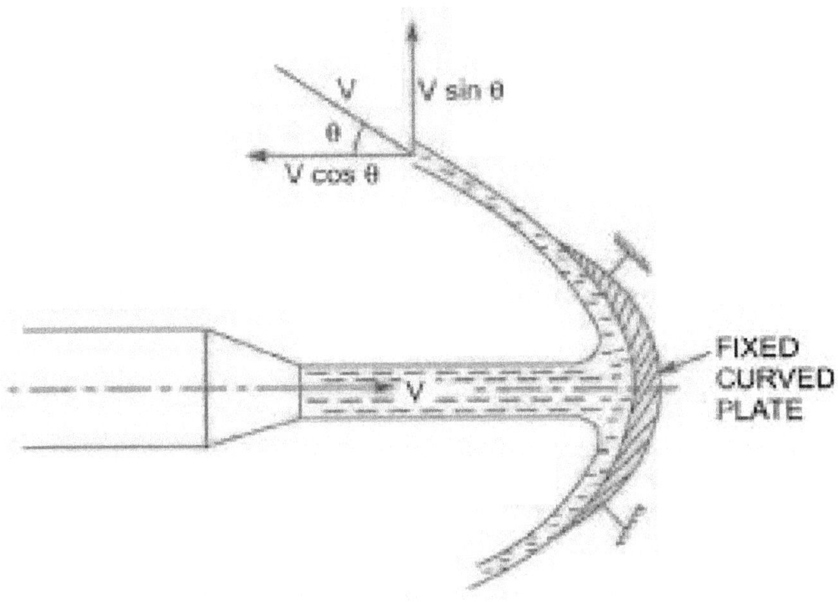

Assumptions

- The plate is smooth and stationary.
- The flow is steady and frictionless.
- There is no loss of energy in the deflection process.
- The jet follows the plate without breaking away.

Force Exerted by Jet (Curved Plate in One Plane)

Let the jet deflect at an angle θ, remaining in one plane (e.g., horizontal plane). The force in the direction of the incoming jet (say, the x-direction) is obtained by the change in momentum :

Initial momentum in x-direction:

$$\dot{m} \cdot V = \rho A V \cdot V = \rho A V^2$$

Final velocity in x-direction:

$$V \cos \theta$$

Final momentum in x-direction:

$$\dot{m} \cdot V \cos \theta = \rho A V \cdot V \cos \theta = \rho A V^2 \cos \theta$$

Change in momentum in x-direction:

$$\rho A V^2 - \rho A V^2 \cos \theta = \rho A V^2 (1 - \cos \theta)$$

Force in the x-direction (F_x) :

$$F_x = \rho A V^2 (1 - \cos \theta)$$

If the **deflection angle** $\theta = 180°$ (i.e., the jet is reversed), then:

$$F_x = \rho A V^2 (1 - \cos 180°) = \rho A V^2 (1 - (-1)) = 2\rho A V^2$$

This is the **maximum force exerted when the jet is reversed.**

Force in the y-direction (F_y) – If Plate Curves Vertically

If the plate also deflects the jet vertically, a component of force arises in the y-direction as well :

$$F_y = \rho A V^2 \sin\theta$$

This is important in 3D curved surfaces, like hemispherical plates or turbine buckets.

Resultant Force
If both x and y components exist, the resultant force is :

$$F_R = \sqrt{F_x^2 + F_y^2}$$

$$F_R = \rho A V^2 \sqrt{(1 - \cos\theta)^2 + \sin^2\theta}$$

Direction of Resultant Force
The direction ϕ of the resultant force with respect to the x-axis is given by :

$$\tan\phi = \frac{F_y}{F_x} = \frac{\sin\theta}{1 - \cos\theta}$$

3.7 Impact of Jet on a Moving Curved Plate

Introduction
When a jet of fluid strikes a curved plate that is moving, the analysis becomes more complex due to the relative motion between the fluid and the plate. This case is important in hydraulic machines such as Pelton wheels, where the buckets (curved plates) move at high speeds and the jet of water

strikes them to transfer momentum and generate power.

Physical Setup

Let the velocity of the jet be V. Let the velocity of the curved plate be uuu, in the same direction as the jet. The plate is smooth and curved, and it moves with constant velocity. The jet strikes tangentially at the center of the curved plate and gets deflected by an angle θ.

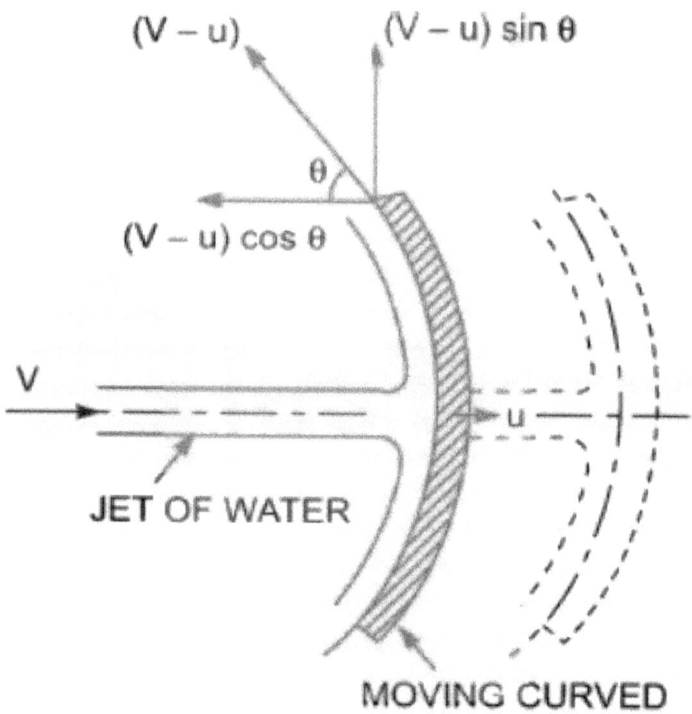

Assumptions

- The flow is steady and incompressible.
- The plate surface is smooth, and there is no energy loss due to friction.
- The jet follows the curvature of the plate perfectly.
- The jet strikes perpendicularly to the motion of the plate (unless specified).

Relative Velocity Concept

To analyze the force exerted on the moving plate, we use the concept of relative velocity:

Relative velocity at inlet = V−u

(Since the jet and plate move in the same direction)

Relative velocity at outlet = V−u

(Magnitude remains same due to frictionless flow)

Force Exerted by Jet on Curved Plate

The mass flow rate striking the plate =

$$\dot{m} = \rho A(V-u)$$

The velocity of water leaving the plate (relative) = V−u, but at an angle θ. Its component along the initial direction of motion (x-direction) = (V−u)cos θ

Initial momentum (in x-direction):

$$\dot{m} \cdot (V - u) = \rho A(V - u)^2$$

Final momentum (in x-direction):

$$\dot{m} \cdot (V - u) \cos \theta = \rho A(V - u)^2 \cos \theta$$

Change in momentum:

$$\rho A(V - u)^2(1 - \cos \theta)$$

Force Exerted on the Plate (F) :

$$F = \rho A(V - u)^2(1 - \cos \theta)$$

This is the force exerted by the jet on the moving curved plate in the direction of motion.

Work Done by the Jet

The work done by the jet on the moving plate per second :

$$W = \text{Force} \times \text{velocity of plate} = F \cdot u = \rho A(V - u)^2(1 - \cos\theta) \cdot u$$

This represents the power transferred from the jet to the plate. It is a key expression in hydraulic turbines.

Efficiency of Jet (η)

Efficiency is the ratio of power developed by the plate to the kinetic energy of the jet :

$$\eta = \frac{\text{Work done per second}}{\text{Initial K.E. of the jet per second}} = \frac{F \cdot u}{\frac{1}{2}\rho A V^3}$$

Using the formula:

$$\eta = \frac{2u(V - u)^2(1 - \cos\theta)}{V^3}$$

This is a generalized expression. If $\theta = 180°$, i.e., full reversal (as in Pelton wheel):

$$F = 2\rho A(V - u)^2 \quad \text{and} \quad \eta = \frac{4u(V - u)^2}{V^3}$$

This is the maximum efficiency condition for a jet striking a symmetrical curved moving plate.

Sample numerical

Q. A jet of water having a velocity of 20 m/s and cross-sectional area 0.02 m² strikes a flat vertical plate held stationary. Calculate the force exerted by the jet on the plate.

Jet velocity, V=20 m/s

Area of jet, A=0.02 m2

Density of water, ρ=1000 kg/m3

Solution:

Discharge

$$Q = A{\cdot}V = 0.02 \times 20 = 0.4 \text{ m3/s}$$

Mass flow rate,

$$\text{m}^\cdot = \rho Q = 1000 \times 0.4 = 400\,\text{kg/s}$$

Force on the plate,

$$F = \text{m}^\cdot \cdot V = 400 \times 20 = 8000\,\text{N}$$

Force = 8000 N

Q. A water jet with velocity 30 m/s and area 0.015 m² strikes a vertical plate moving in the same direction at 10 m/s. Find the force exerted on the plate.

V=30 m/s

u=10 m/s

A=0.015 m2

ρ=1000 kg/m3

Solution:

Relative velocity

$$V_{rel} = V - u = 30 - 10 = 20\,\text{m/s}$$

Mass flow rate

$$\dot{m} = \rho A V_{rel} = 1000 \times 0.015 \times 20 = 300\,\text{kg/s}$$

Force on plate

$$F = \dot{m}(V - u) = 300 \times 20 = 6000\,\text{N}$$

Force = 6000 N

Q. A jet of water of diameter 0.05 m strikes a stationary inclined flat plate at 30° to the jet direction. The jet velocity is 25 m/s. Find the force in the direction of the jet.

d=0.05 m $\Rightarrow$ A = π x d2/4= 0.001963 m2

V=25 m/s

θ=30°

ρ=1000 kg/m3

Mass flow rate,

$$m˙ = \rho AV = 1000 \times 0.001963 \times 25 = 49.08 \text{ kg/s}$$

Force in the direction of jet:

$$F = \dot{m} \cdot V \cdot \cos^2 \theta = 49.08 \cdot 25 \cdot \cos^2(30°)$$

$$\cos(30°) = \frac{\sqrt{3}}{2} \approx 0.866 \Rightarrow \cos^2(30°) \approx 0.75$$

$$F = 49.08 \cdot 25 \cdot 0.75 = 919.13 \text{ N}$$

Force = 919.13 N

CHAPTER FOUR

HYDRAULIC TURBINE

4.1 Basics Of hydroelectric power plant

Introduction to Hydroelectric Power Plant

A hydroelectric power plant is a facility that converts the potential energy of stored water into mechanical energy, and then into electrical energy using a turbine-generator system. It is one of the cleanest and most reliable forms of renewable energy.

Working Principle

The plant works on the principle of converting the energy of water into electricity through the these stages : Potential energy of water stored at height (in a dam or reservoir) is used. As water flows down, it gains kinetic energy. This high-velocity water strikes the blades of a turbine, causing it to rotate. The turbine shaft is connected to an electric generator, which converts mechanical energy into electrical energy. This process is based on the law of conservation of energy — energy cannot be created or destroyed but only converted from one form to another.

Main Components of Hydroelectric power plant

Reservoir - Stores water at a height to create potential energy

Dam - Blocks the river and helps create the reservoir

Penstock - A large pipe that carries water from the reservoir to the turbine

Turbine - Converts the kinetic energy of water into mechanical energy

Generator - Converts mechanical energy into electrical energy

Draft Tube - Discharges water from turbine to tailrace at lower pressure

Tailrace - Channel that carries water away from the turbine back to the river

Control Gate / Valve - Regulates the flow of water to the turbine

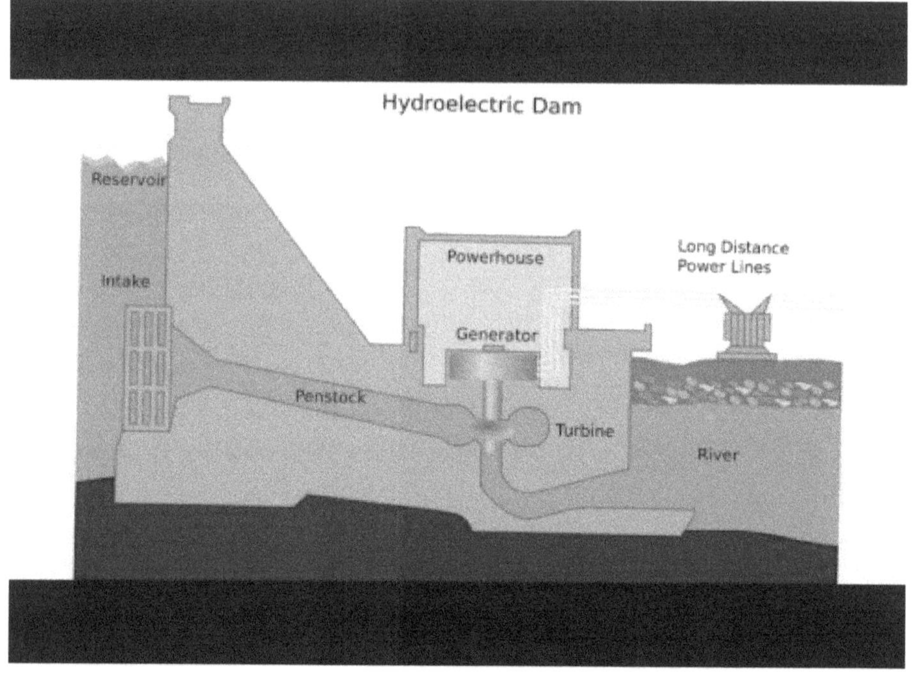

Layout of a Hydroelectric Power Plant

Advantages of Hydroelectric Power

- Renewable and non-polluting source of energy
- High efficiency (up to 90%)
- Low operating and maintenance cost
- Can be started and stopped quickly
- Provides water for irrigation and flood control (dual-purpose dams)

Disadvantages

- High initial cost of dam and plant construction
- Large land area is submerged
- Affects local ecosystems and wildlife
- Depends on seasonal rainfall

4.2 classification of hydraulic turbine

Based on Type of Energy at Inlet

a) Impulse Turbine

Uses kinetic energy of water only. Water strikes the turbine blades in the form of high-velocity jets. Pressure remains constant throughout the turbine. Suitable for high-head applications. Example: Pelton Wheel.

b) Reaction Turbine

Uses both pressure energy and kinetic energy of water.Water flows over the blades and pressure changes during flow. Requires casing and draft tube. Examples: Francis Turbine, Kaplan Turbine.

Based on Head (Height of Water Above Turbine)

a) High Head

When water head above turbine is more than 100 m. Example Pelton wheel .

b) Medium Head

When water head above turbine is in between 30m to 100 m. Example Francis Turbine.

C) Low Head

When water head above turbine is lees than 30 m. Example Kaplaan Turbine.

Based on Direction of Flow Through Runner

a) Tangetial flow

When water from penstock strike tangetially to blade of turbine. Example Pelton wheel.

b) Radial Flow

When water from penstock strike radially to blade or perpendicular to shaft of turbine. Example Francis turbine (old design).

c) Axial flow

When water from penstock flow parallel to shaft of turbine. Example kaplan turbine.

d) Mixed flow

Water enters radially in turbine and exits axially from turbine. Example Modern francis turbine.

Based on Specific Speed

a) Low Specific Speed

When specific speed of turbine strike in between 10 rpm to 35 rpm. Example Pelton wheel.

b) Medium Specific Speed

When specific speed of turbine strike in between 60 rpm to 300 rpm. Example Francis turbine.

c) High Specific Speed

When specific speed of turbine strike above 300 rpm. Example kaplan turbine.

4.2.1 Various factor affecting selecttion of hydraulic turbine

The performance and efficiency of a hydroelectric power plant largely depend on the correct selection of a hydraulic turbine. Several technical and environmental factors must be considered to ensure that the turbine operates efficiently under site-specific conditions.

Available Head

The head is the vertical distance between the water source and the turbine.It directly affects the type of turbine to be selected.

Discharge (Flow Rate)

The volume of water available per second (in m^3/s) influences turbine choice.High discharge with low head requires turbines like Kaplan, while low discharge with high head is suitable for Pelton.

Specific Speed of Turbine (Ns)

Determines turbine suitability based on head and power output.Helps compare performance and select turbine type.

Site Conditions and Layout

Vertical or horizontal shaft orientation is selected based on site layout and installation constraints. Limited space may require horizontal shaft turbines, while large power plants prefer vertical arrangements.

Efficiency Requirements

Different turbines offer different maximum efficiencies at varying heads and discharges. Efficiency is crucial for maximizing output and reducing energy losses.

Variation in Load Demand

If the load varies frequently, the turbine must maintain performance at partial load. Francis turbines are best suited for moderate load variations. Kaplan turbines handle large load fluctuations effectively due to adjustable blades.

Cost and Maintenance

Initial cost, operating cost, and ease of maintenance must be considered. Pelton turbines are simpler and easier to maintain. Kaplan turbines, though more efficient at low heads, are costlier and complex.

Cavitation Consideration

Cavitation is the formation of vapor bubbles due to pressure drop, which damages turbine blades. Turbines must be selected with suitable design and materials to minimize cavitation risks. Kaplan and Francis turbines are more prone to cavitation than Pelton wheels.

Environmental Impact

Low-head turbines (like Kaplan) may require large flooded areas. Site-specific environmental concerns (like submergence, aquatic life, etc.) may limit certain turbine types.

4.3 Pelton wheel turbine

Introduction

The Pelton wheel is an impulse-type hydraulic turbine used primarily for high-head, low-flow applications. It operates by converting the kinetic energy of a water jet into mechanical energy through the impulse action on specially shaped buckets mounted on a rotating wheel.

Construction of Pelton Wheel

A Pelton wheel consists of the following main components :

Nozzle and Spear - Converts pressure energy of water into a high-velocity jet; spear regulates flow.

Runner - Circular disc mounted on a shaft that holds the buckets

Buckets (Blades) - Double hemispherical cups that split the jet into two halves and extract kinetic energy

Casing - Encloses the turbine to prevent water splashing and direct it to the tailrace

Shaft - Transmits mechanical energy from runner to generator

Brake Nozzle - Stops the runner quickly after shutting off water flow

Tailrace - Channel through which used water is discharged

Each Pelton bucket has a central ridge (splitter) that divides the incoming jet into two equal parts, allowing water to flow smoothly and efficiently along the inner curves of the bucket, reducing energy loss.

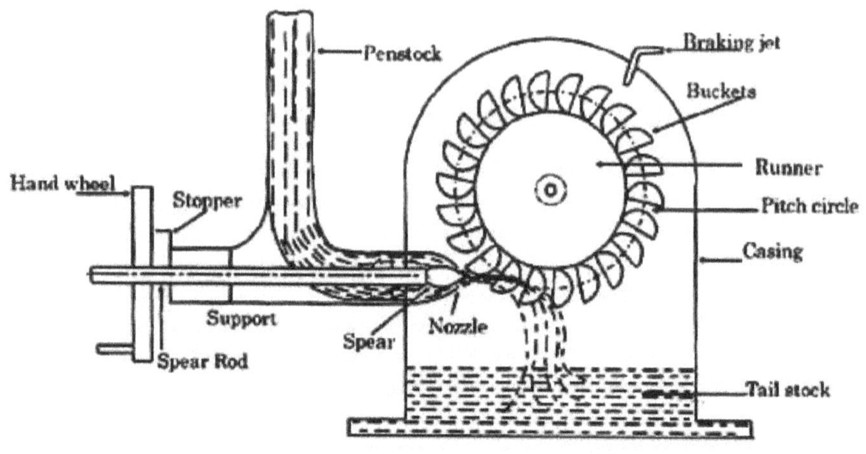

Pelton wheel turbine

Working Principle

The Pelton wheel operates on the impulse principle : "All available head is converted into kinetic energy in the form of a high-speed water jet, which then strikes the turbine's buckets and produces torque."

Step-by-Step Process:

- Water is stored in a high-altitude reservoir (creating high potential energy).
- It flows through a penstock (long pipe) to the nozzle, where its pressure energy is fully converted into kinetic energy forming a high-velocity jet.
- This jet is directed tangentially onto the buckets of the Pelton wheel.
- As the jet hits the splitter in the bucket, it splits and flows around the curves, exerting an impulse force.
- The force causes the runner to rotate, thereby converting water's kinetic energy into mechanical energy.
- The used water falls into the tailrace, and the rotating shaft drives the electrical generator to produce electricity.

Advantages of Pelton Wheel

- High efficiency at high heads
- Simple design and easy maintenance
- Can be operated at high rotational speeds
- Can handle large head variations

Limitations

- Not suitable for low head or high discharge applications
- Bulky at low head due to large size runner and buckets
- Needs high-quality water (free of debris) to avoid erosion

Application Areas

- High-head hydroelectric power stations
- Mountainous or hilly regions (e.g., Himachal Pradesh, Uttarakhand)
- Remote mini hydro plants

4.4 Francis Turbine

Introduction

The Francis turbine is a widely used reaction-type hydraulic turbine that operates efficiently under medium head and moderate discharge conditions. It is a mixed-flow turbine, meaning water enters radially and exits axially. This design provides high efficiency, making it ideal for large hydroelectric power plants.

Construction of Francis Turbine

The Francis turbine consists of the following major components :

Spiral Casing (Scroll Casing) - Uniformly distributes water around the turbine runner

Stay Vanes - Support the guide vanes and direct flow toward them

Guide Vanes (Wicket Gates) - Control the flow rate and angle of water entering the runner

Runner - Rotating part with curved blades that converts water energy into mechanical energy

Runner Blades - Receive water flow and rotate the runner using both pressure and velocity forces

Draft Tube - Expands to reduce velocity and recover pressure before discharging water

Shaft - Transmits mechanical energy from runner to generator

The spiral casing ensures water enters all guide vanes uniformly. The guide vanes are adjustable, allowing flow regulation even during operation. The runner blades are curved, suited for both radial entry and axial exit of water.

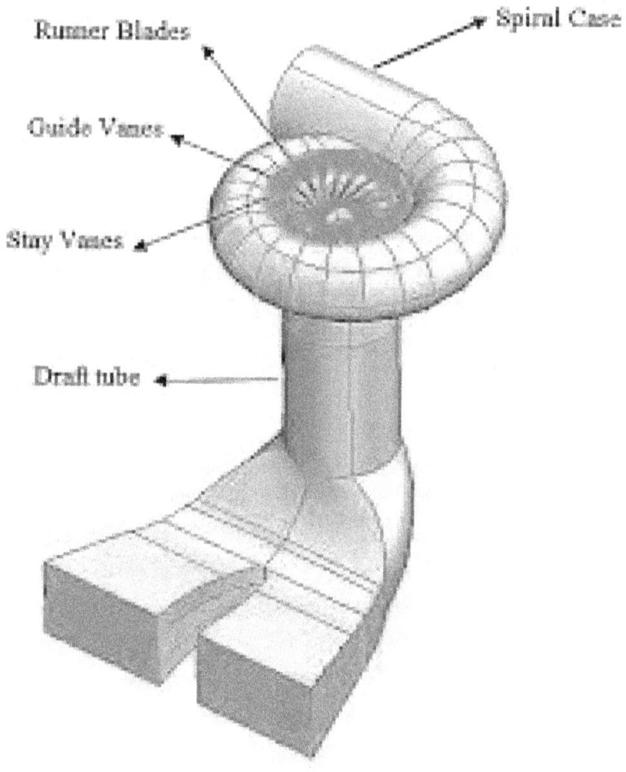

Francis turbine

Working Principle

The Francis turbine works on the principle of a reaction turbine — it utilizes both the pressure energy and the kinetic energy of water to develop torque.

Working Process:

- Water from the penstock enters the spiral casing, which surrounds the turbine runner.
- The water passes through stay vanes and guide vanes, which direct the flow at a proper angle to the runner blades.
- The water enters the runner radially and is guided by the blades to exit axially.
- As water passes over the curved blades, it loses pressure and velocity, causing the runner to rotate.
- The rotating shaft transmits mechanical energy to the generator.
- Water then enters the draft tube, where velocity is reduced and pressure is partially recovered before being discharged into the tailrace.

Flow Path (Mixed Flow)

- Radial entry: Water enters the runner perpendicularly to the shaft axis.
- Axial exit: Water leaves the runner parallel to the shaft axis.
- This combination allows better pressure recovery and efficient energy transfer.

Advantages of Francis Turbine

- High efficiency (90–94%)
- Operates well over a wide range of heads (30–100 m)
- Compact and suitable for large-scale power generation
- Can handle variable flow with adjustable guide vanes

Limitations

- Sensitive to cavitation
- Requires complex manufacturing and precise alignment
- Less suitable for very high or very low head applications

Application Areas

- Medium-head hydroelectric power stations
- Base-load stations requiring continuous operation

- Large dams like Bhakra Nangal (India)

4.5 Kaplan turbine

Introduction

The Kaplan turbine is an axial flow reaction turbine, specifically designed for low-head and high-discharge hydroelectric applications. It is similar in principle to the propeller but includes adjustable blades, allowing high efficiency even under varying loads and flow conditions. Invented by Viktor Kaplan in 1913, it is widely used in large low-head power stations.

Construction of Kaplan Turbine

Spiral Casing - Delivers water uniformly to guide vanes around the runner

Guide Vanes (Wicket Gates) - Control flow rate and direction of water entering the runner

Runner (with adjustable blades) - Converts water energy into rotational motion; blades adjust to flow conditions

Hub (Blade Control Mechanism) - Mechanically controls the angle of runner blades during operation

Shaft - Transfers torque from runner to generator

Draft Tube - Recovers pressure and directs water to the tailrace

Tailrace - Channel where water is discharged after energy extraction

The runner blades in Kaplan turbines are adjustable (pitch-controlled), unlike fixed-blade propeller turbines. This allows optimal performance under part-load and full-load conditions.

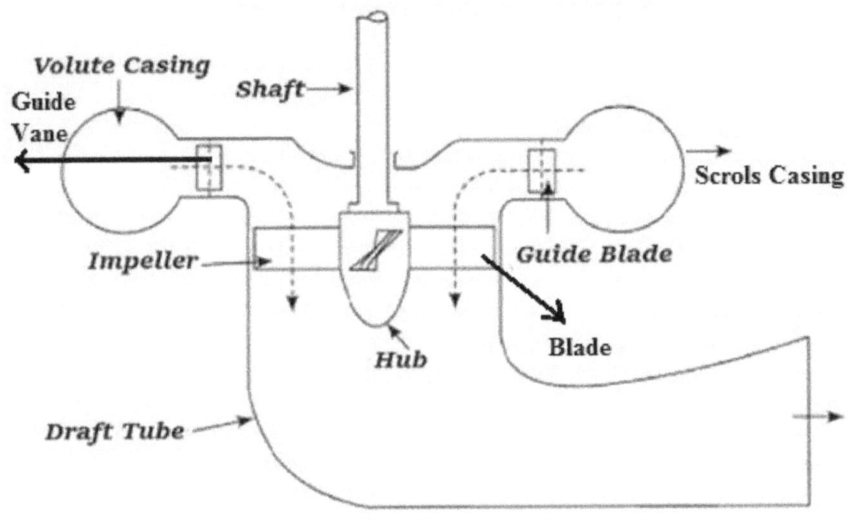

Kaplan turbine

Working Principle

Kaplan turbine works on the reaction principle, using both pressure and kinetic energy of water to generate mechanical energy.

Step-by-Step Working:

- Water from the penstock enters the spiral casing, surrounding the runner.
- It flows through guide vanes, which adjust to control water flow and direct it at the correct angle.
- Water enters the runner blades axially, i.e., along the shaft direction.
- As water passes through the adjustable runner blades, it exerts force and causes the runner to rotate.
- The rotating shaft drives the generator to produce electricity.
- Water exits through the draft tube, where its velocity reduces and pressure is partially recovered.

Flow Path

- Axial Flow: Water flows parallel to the turbine shaft from entry to exit.

- Both guide vanes and runner blades are adjustable to maintain high efficiency at variable loads.

Advantages of Kaplan Turbine

- High efficiency over a wide range of loads
- Ideal for low-head (2–30 m) and high-flow conditions
- Adjustable blades ensure constant efficiency even at variable water flow
- Compact design with vertical mounting possible

Limitations

- Mechanically complex (blade adjustment mechanism)
- Higher initial cost and maintenance
- Sensitive to cavitation

Applications

- Low-head hydroelectric power plants
- Run-of-the-river projects
- Tidal power stations

4.6 Draft tube

Introduction

A draft tube is an enlarging conduit (gradually expanding pipe) connected to the outlet of a reaction turbine. Its purpose is to discharge water from the runner to the tailrace and recover a portion of the kinetic energy of the flow exiting the turbine.

The draft tube is essential for the efficient operation of reaction turbines like Francis and Kaplan, which operate under pressure below atmospheric level at the runner exit.

Functions of a Draft Tube

- Reduces velocity of water exiting the runner, thereby converting kinetic energy into pressure energy (energy recovery).

- Lifts water to the tailrace level even when the turbine is installed above it.
- Maintains continuous flow through the turbine by creating a suction head.
- Prevents the entry of air into the turbine casing.
- Increases the net head available to the turbine.

Principle of Operation

Draft tube works based on Bernoulli's equation and the concept of energy conversion : As water flows through the enlarging section of the draft tube, its velocity decreases. According to Bernoulli's principle, the pressure increases (partial recovery of kinetic energy). This recovered pressure energy contributes to improved turbine efficiency.

Types of Draft Tubes

a) Conical Draft Tube (Straight Divergent Tube)

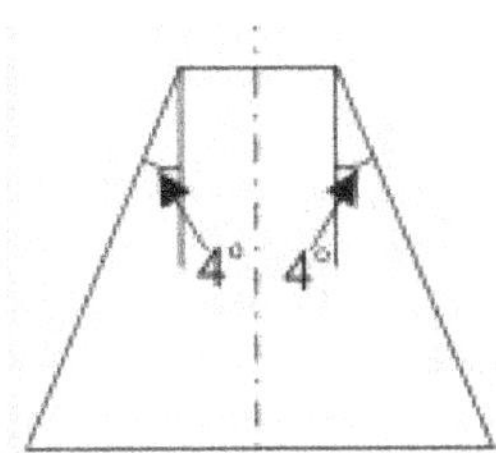

Gradually diverging pipe.
Typically used in vertical Francis turbines.
Best efficiency due to gradual deceleration of flow.

b) Simple Elbow Draft Tube

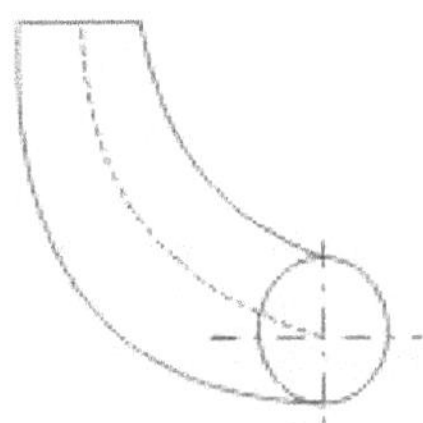

Elbow-shaped tube with horizontal outlet.
Suitable where vertical space is limited.

Commonly used in Kaplan turbines.

c) Moody's Spreading Draft Tube (Elbow with Circular to Rectangular Transition)

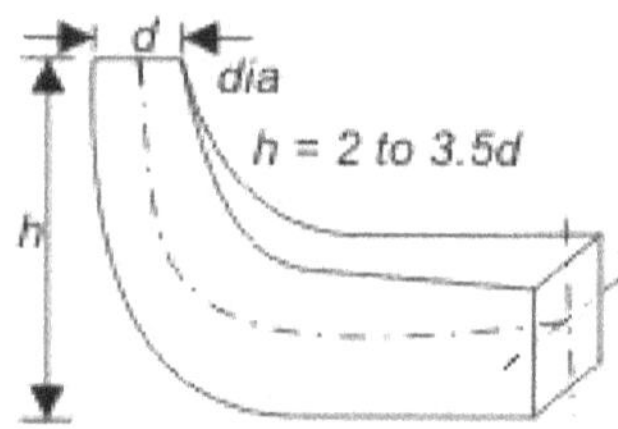

An elbow draft tube with a gradually expanding cross-section. Converts circular pipe flow to rectangular or trapezoidal channel. Installed in powerhouses with limited floor space.

d) Draft tube circular inlet and rectangular outlet

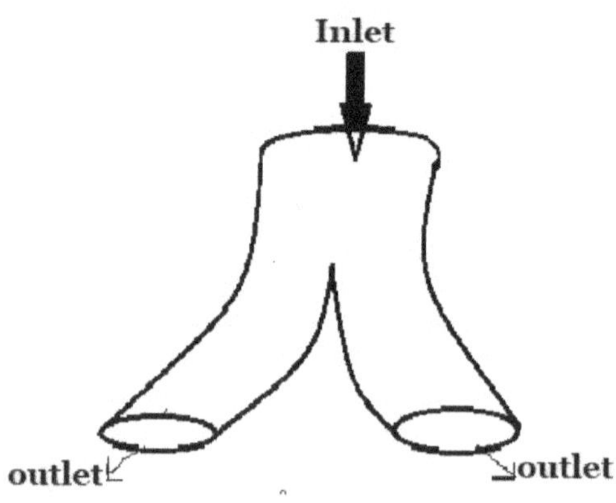

Inlet of this draft tube is circular
outlet of this ddraf tube is recangular
Provides smooth flow with minimal energy loss.

The draft tube is an essential component in reaction turbines, contributing significantly to overall efficiency and energy recovery. Proper design ensures smoother flow, reduced losses, and improved net power output.

4.7 Cavitation in Hydraulic Turbines

What is Cavitation?

Cavitation is a phenomenon in which vapor bubbles form in a flowing liquid when the local pressure falls below the vapor pressure of the fluid, and these bubbles collapse violently when they move into high-pressure zones. In hydraulic turbines, this occurs mainly in the runner and draft tube where pressure is low.

Where Cavitation Occurs in Turbines

Francis Turbine: At the runner exit or in the draft tube, Kaplan Turbine: On the suction side of blades, Pelton Wheel: On the bucket surface near jet impact area (less frequent)

Causes of Cavitation

Low pressure in draft tube - Pressure may fall below vapor pressure, especially at high flow velocities

High suction head - Excessive height between turbine and tailrace increases cavitation risk

Improper turbine setting - Incorrect elevation of turbine above tailwater level

Sudden changes in flow direction - Create local pressure drops and turbulence

High flow velocity - Increases kinetic energy, reducing static pressure below vapor pressure

Effects of Cavitation

Pitting of surfaces - Erosion and surface damage of blades and runner due to bubble collapse

Vibration and noise - Unsteady collapse of vapor bubbles causes noise and mechanical vibrations

Reduced efficiency - Energy is lost in bubble formation and collapse

Structural failure - Long-term cavitation can weaken or fracture turbine parts

Increased maintenance cost - Due to frequent repair or replacement of damaged parts

Prevention of Cavitation

a) Proper Installation Height (Turbine Setting)

Install the turbine as low as possible relative to the tailwater level to keep pressure above vapor pressure. Ensure Net Positive Suction Head (NPSH) is adequate.

b) Use of Draft Tube

A well-designed draft tube increases the pressure recovery and reduces the risk of cavitation by avoiding sharp pressure drops.

c) Smooth Blade Design

Use streamlined, polished blades to minimize flow separation and sharp pressure drops.

d) Material Selection

Use cavitation-resistant materials (like stainless steel or hard alloys) for runner blades and other critical parts.

e) Air Admission

In some turbines, controlled air is admitted to reduce suction pressure and avoid low-pressure zones.

f) Operation within Design Limits

Avoid operating the turbine under extreme part-load or overload conditions.

4.8 Calculation of Work Done, Power, and Efficiency of Turbines

Understanding how to calculate the work output, power generated, and efficiency of a hydraulic turbine is essential for analyzing turbine performance and selecting the appropriate equipment for a hydroelectric system.

Work Done by a Turbine

The work done by water on the turbine runner is based on the principle of momentum change. According to Euler's Equation for Turbines :

$$\text{Work done per unit weight of water} = \frac{V_{w1}u_1 - V_{w2}u_2}{g}$$

Vw1 = Whirl component of absolute velocity at inlet
Vw2 = Whirl component of absolute velocity at outlet
u = Peripheral velocity of runner at inlet and outlet
g = Acceleration due to gravity (9.81 m/s²)

Power Developed by the Turbine

$$\text{Power}(P) = \rho Q (V_{w1} u_1 - V_{w2} u_2)$$

ρ = Density of water (1000 kg/m³)
Q = Discharge through the turbine (m³/s)
Units:
P is in watts (W) or kilowatts (kW)

Efficiency of Turbines

a) Hydraulic Efficiency (η_h)

$$\eta_h = \frac{\text{Power developed by runner}}{\text{Water power supplied}} = \frac{\rho Q (V_{w1} u_1 - V_{w2} u_2)}{\rho g Q H} = \frac{(V_{w1} u_1 - V_{w2} u_2)}{g H}$$

b) Mechanical Efficiency (η_m)

$$\eta_m = \frac{\text{Shaft Power}}{\text{Power developed by runner}}$$

Accounts for mechanical losses in bearings, friction, etc.

c) Overall Efficiency (η_o)

$$\eta_o = \frac{\text{Shaft Power}}{\text{Water Power}} = \eta_h \times \eta_m$$

Overall efficiency reflects the true performance of the turbine from input to useful output.

Example
Discharge, Q = 2.5 m3/s

Head, H=60 m

Turbine output power = 1200 kW

Then:

Water power = WP = ρgQH = 1000×9.81×2.5×60 = 1,471,500 W = 1471.5 kW

Overall efficiency

$$\eta_o = \frac{1200}{1471.5} \approx 81.5\%$$

4.9 Hydraulic Ram

Introduction

A hydraulic ram (or hydram) is a reciprocating water pump that uses the energy of falling water (low head, high discharge) to lift a small quantity of water to a higher elevation. It is a simple and eco-friendly device that works without any external power source, making it ideal for rural and remote areas.

Principle of Operation

The hydraulic ram works on the principle of the water hammer effect. Water hammer is a pressure surge caused when flowing water is suddenly stopped or forced to change direction. The hydram uses the kinetic energy of a large quantity of water flowing from a low head to lift a small portion of that water to a higher head.

Main Components of a Hydraulic Ram

Drive Pipe - Delivers water from the source to the pump

Waste Valve (Impulse Valve) - Opens initially to allow water flow, then closes suddenly to create water hammer

Delivery Valve (Check Valve) - Opens due to pressure rise and allows water to flow into the delivery pipe

Air Chamber - Absorbs pressure surges and provides a smooth flow

Delivery Pipe - Carries water to the higher elevation storage

Pump Body - Cast housing that contains the valves and air chamber

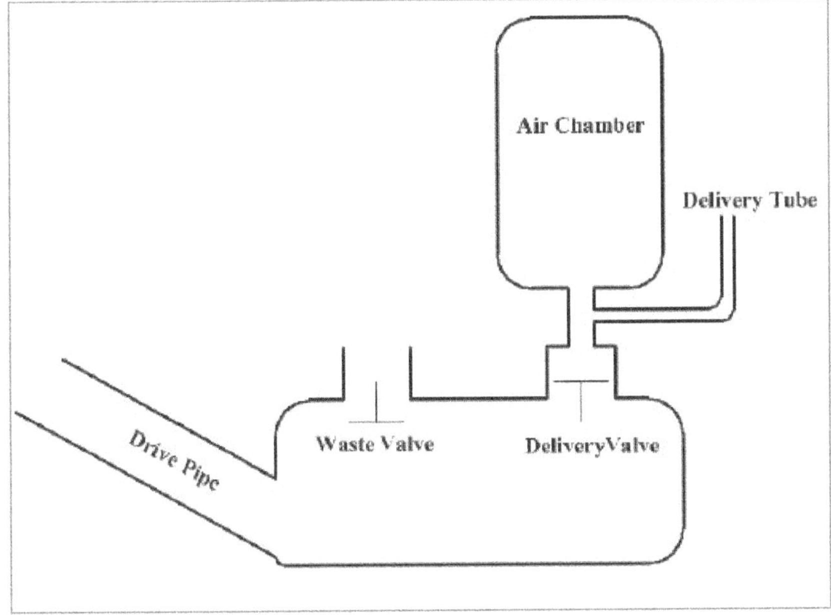

Hydraulic Ram

Working of Hydraulic Ram

Initial Flow - Water from the source flows through the drive pipe and exits through the waste valve, which is open initially.

Sudden Closure of Waste Valve - As water picks up speed, its momentum closes the waste valve suddenly, creating a high-pressure spike due to water hammer.

Opening of Delivery Valve - The pressure rise opens the delivery valve, and a small portion of water enters the air chamber and is pushed into the delivery pipe.

Pressure Drops - Once the water slows, pressure drops and the delivery valve closes.

Waste Valve Reopens - The cycle restarts as the waste valve opens under falling pressure, and the process repeats automatically.

Advantages

- Uses no external power

- Simple and durable design
- Ideal for hilly and remote areas
- Minimal operational cost

Limitations

- Requires continuous flow of water from a source
- Only a small percentage of water is lifted
- Not suitable for high-volume water supply

4.10 Hydraulic press

Introduction

A hydraulic press is a device used to lift or compress heavy loads by applying a small force over a large area using the principle of Pascal's Law. It is widely used in industries for molding, forging, pressing, punching, and other high-force applications.

Principle of Hydraulic Press – Pascal's Law

Pascal's Law:

"The pressure applied to a confined fluid is transmitted undiminished in all directions."

This means that a small force applied to a small area can generate a large force on a larger area, if both areas are connected through a fluid (usually oil or water).

Construction of a Hydraulic Press

Plunger (Small Piston) - Where the input force is applied manually or by a pump

Cylinder (Small) - Holds the plunger and transmits pressure to the fluid

Ram (Large Piston) - Moves upward to lift or compress the load

Cylinder (Large) - Contains the ram and receives fluid under pressure

Working Fluid - Usually oil or water that transmits pressure

Valves - Control the flow of fluid between cylinders and reservoir

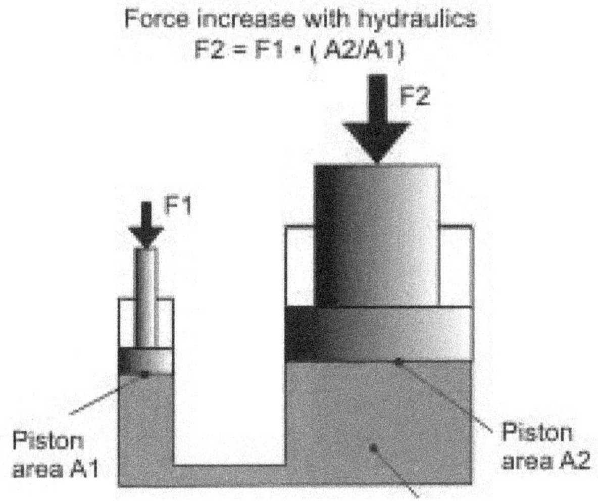

Enter Caption

Working of Hydraulic Press

- A small force F1 is applied to the plunger (area A1).
- According to Pascal's Law, the pressure P=F1/A1 is transmitted throughout the fluid.
- This pressure acts on the ram (area A2) to produce a larger force F2=P·A2.
- As a result, the ram moves upward, lifting or compressing the load.

Formulae and Calculation

Pressure Applied:

$$P = \frac{F_1}{A_1}$$

Force Exerted by Ram:

$$F_2 = P \cdot A_2 = \frac{F_1 \cdot A_2}{A_1}$$

Mechanical Advantage (M.A.):

$$M.A. = \frac{F_2}{F_1} = \frac{A_2}{A_1}$$

Thus, the force is amplified based on the ratio of areas of the ram and the plunger.

Applications of Hydraulic Press

- Automobile workshops (car lifts)
- Sheet metal forming and pressing
- Compression of bales (cotton, paper, etc.)
- Molding and forging operations
- Plastic and rubber product manufacturing

Advantages

- Can lift or press very heavy loads with minimal input force
- Smooth and controlled operation
- Requires less space for large force generation
- Durable and reliable in industrial use

Limitations

- Slow operation compared to mechanical presses
- Hydraulic oil may leak and cause maintenance issues
- Requires careful pressure control to avoid system damage

4.11 Hydraulic Intensifier

Introduction

A hydraulic intensifier is a device used to increase the pressure of a fluid (usually water or oil) by using energy from a low-pressure, high-flow fluid. It is commonly used where high-pressure fluid is needed intermittently, such as in hydraulic presses, cutting tools, and clamping systems.

Purpose

Many hydraulic systems require high-pressure fluid for operation, but generating high pressure directly from a pump may not be efficient or feasible. A hydraulic intensifier solves this by converting low-pressure energy into high-pressure output, efficiently and economically.

Principle of Operation

The hydraulic intensifier works based on Pascal's Law and conservation of energy:

"In a confined fluid system, the pressure applied is transmitted equally in all directions."

It uses the force balance between two pistons of different areas:

Since Force = Pressure × Area, (Smaller piston generates higher pressure).

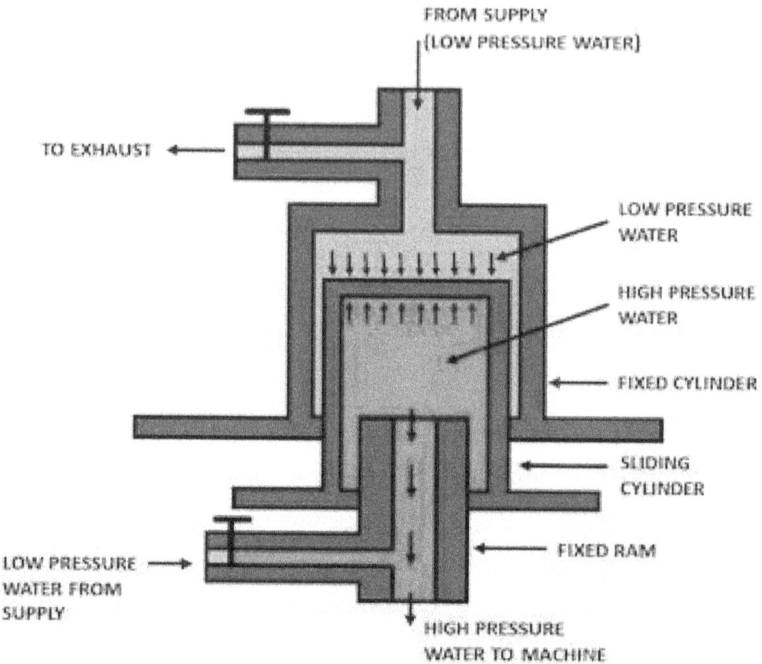

Hydraulic intensifier

Construction of Hydraulic Intensifier

Low-pressure cylinder - Receives fluid from a pump at low pressure

Low-pressure piston - Large diameter piston that moves inward and pushes high-pressure piston

High-pressure cylinder - Contains fluid to be intensified

High-pressure piston - Smaller piston that builds up high pressure

Inlet/Outlet Valves - Regulate the flow of fluid during operation

Water or oil reservoir - Stores low-pressure fluid

Working of Hydraulic Intensifier

Low-pressure fluid enters the large cylinder, pushing the large piston forward. This movement compresses the high-pressure piston inside a smaller cylinder. Since pressure is inversely proportional to area

$$\frac{P_2}{P_1} = \frac{A_1}{A_2}$$

P1 = Low pressure

P2 = High pressure

A1, A2 = Areas of low-pressure and high-pressure pistons

The result is a high-pressure fluid output used for downstream operations like presses or clamping.

Applications

- Hydraulic presses
- Machine tool operations (clamping, punching)
- Hydraulic jacks
- High-pressure cutting or forming systems
- Aircraft and automotive hydraulic systems

Advantages

- Produces high pressure from low-pressure input
- Compact and simple in construction
- Useful in intermittent high-pressure systems
- Reduces need for large high-pressure pumps

Limitations

- Not suitable for continuous high-pressure operation
- Pressure build-up is intermittent (in cycles)
- Limited volume of high-pressure fluid per cycle

4.12 Hydraulic accumulator

Introduction

A hydraulic accumulator is a device used to store hydraulic energy in the form of pressurized fluid. It supplies high-pressure fluid on demand, especially during peak loads or sudden requirements, and helps maintain system pressure and efficiency. Think of it as a battery for a hydraulic system — storing energy when not needed and releasing it when required.

Purpose of Hydraulic Accumulator

Stores excess energy from the pump during low-load conditions. Supplies high-pressure fluid instantly during peak load or emergency operation. Maintains constant pressure in the hydraulic system. Helps in shock absorption and vibration control. Reduces the size and power rating required for pumps.

Principle of Operation

The hydraulic accumulator works on Pascal's Law and potential energy storage:

A small amount of fluid under high pressure is stored in the accumulator using a heavy weight, spring, or compressed gas to maintain that pressure.

When the system requires energy, The accumulator discharges fluid into the system. When the load is low, The pump refills the accumulator for the next cycle.

Construction of a Simple Weight-Loaded Accumulator
Vertical Cylinder - Holds hydraulic fluid
Sliding Ram or Piston - Moves vertically due to fluid pressure
Weight - Applies downward force to maintain pressure
Fluid Inlet/Outlet - Allows entry and exit of pressurized fluid
Guide Rods - Keep the piston aligned during operation

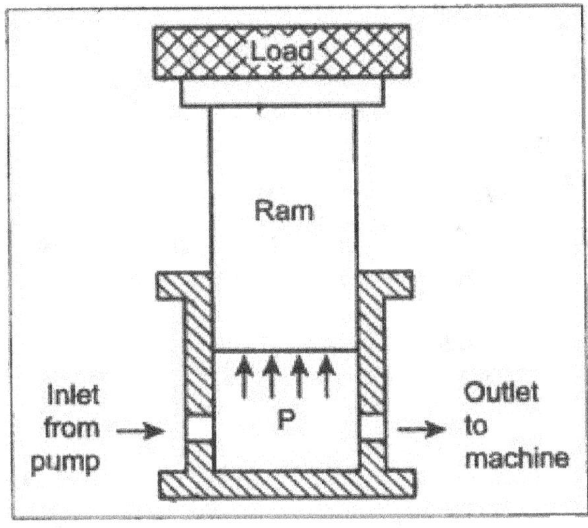

Hydraulic accumulator

Working of a Hydraulic Accumulator
Charging Phase:
Pump sends pressurized fluid into the accumulator. The ram or piston moves upward, lifting the weight (or compressing spring/gas).
Storing Phase:
The fluid is stored under pressure and held in readiness.
Discharging Phase:
When the system demands more fluid (e.g., during operation of a hydraulic press), the stored fluid is released under pressure, supplementing the pump.
Applications

- Hydraulic presses and lifts
- Injection molding machines
- Machine tools
- Aircraft hydraulic systems
- Load holding and balancing
- Emergency systems (e.g., for brakes, doors)

Advantages

- Provides immediate high-pressure fluid
- Reduces size and power requirement of pumps
- Improves response time and system stability
- Absorbs shocks and pulsations

Limitations

- Limited storage capacity
- Needs safety systems to prevent overpressure
- Maintenance required for seals and moving parts

CHAPTER FIVE

PUMPS

5.1 Pumps

Introduction

In many engineering systems, it is necessary to transport fluids (usually water or oil) from one place to another, sometimes against gravity or pressure differences. This is where pumps are used.

A pump is a mechanical device that moves fluids from a lower pressure region to a higher pressure region, usually by adding mechanical energy to the fluid. Pumps are widely used in households, agriculture, industries, and hydraulic machines.

A pump is a machine used to transfer or raise the level of a fluid by converting mechanical energy into hydraulic energy. It increases the pressure of the fluid to help it flow through pipelines, systems, or over elevations. Pumps require external power sources such as electric motors, engines, or human effort.

5.1.1 Applications of Pumps

Domestic Applications

- Lifting water from wells or underground tanks
- Circulating water in cooling/heating systems
- Supplying water to overhead tanks

Agricultural Applications

- Irrigation (lift irrigation and sprinkler systems)
- Draining flooded lands

Industrial Applications

- Cooling water circulation in power plants
- Transferring oils, chemicals, or fluids in refineries and factories
- Hydraulic systems in presses and jacks

Civil and Municipal Uses

- Water supply to cities and towns
- Sewage and drainage pumping stations

Marine and Automotive

- Fuel and oil transfer in ships and vehicles
- Bilge pumping on boats

5.1.2. Classification of pumps

Pumps are classified based on working principle, fluid flow direction, construction, and application. This classification helps in selecting the appropriate pump for specific engineering needs.

Based on Principle of Operation

a) Positive Displacement Pumps

These pumps trap a fixed volume of fluid and then force it through the discharge pipe. They deliver a fixed amount of fluid per cycle, regardless of system pressure.

- Reciprocating Pump
- Rotary Pump

b) Dynamic (Rotodynamic) Pumps

These pumps impart kinetic energy to the fluid using a rotating impeller. The velocity is later converted into pressure.

- Centrifugal Pump
- Axial Flow Pump
- Mixed Flow Pump

Based on Direction of Flow
a) Radial FlowFluid (Centrifugal pump)
b) Axial FlowFluid (Propeller pump)
c) Mixed Flow (Mixed-flow pump)
Based on Number of Stages
a) Single-Stage (One impeller/piston)
b) Multi-StageMultiple (impellers/pistons in series)

5.2 Centrifugal pump

Introduction

A centrifugal pump is the most commonly used type of dynamic (rotodynamic) pump. It works on the principle of centrifugal force, which converts mechanical energy into hydraulic energy (pressure head). It is widely used for pumping water in homes, farms, industries, and municipal water supply systems.

Principle of Operation

The centrifugal pump works on the principle of centrifugal force:

"When a mass of liquid is rotated, it is thrown outward from the center by centrifugal force. This increases the pressure energy of the fluid."

The pump imparts kinetic energy to the fluid using a rotating impeller, which is later converted into pressure energy in the volute casing.

Construction of Centrifugal Pump

Impeller - A rotating wheel with vanes that imparts velocity to the fluid

Casing (Volute) - Spiral-shaped enclosure that collects the fluid and converts velocity into pressure

Suction Pipe with Foot Valve and Strainer - Draws liquid from the sump into the pump

Delivery Pipe - Delivers the pressurized liquid to the required location

Pump Shaft - Connects impeller to motor and transmits mechanical power

Bearings and Glands - Support and seal the shaft to prevent leakage

Priming Plug - Used to fill the casing with water before starting (priming)

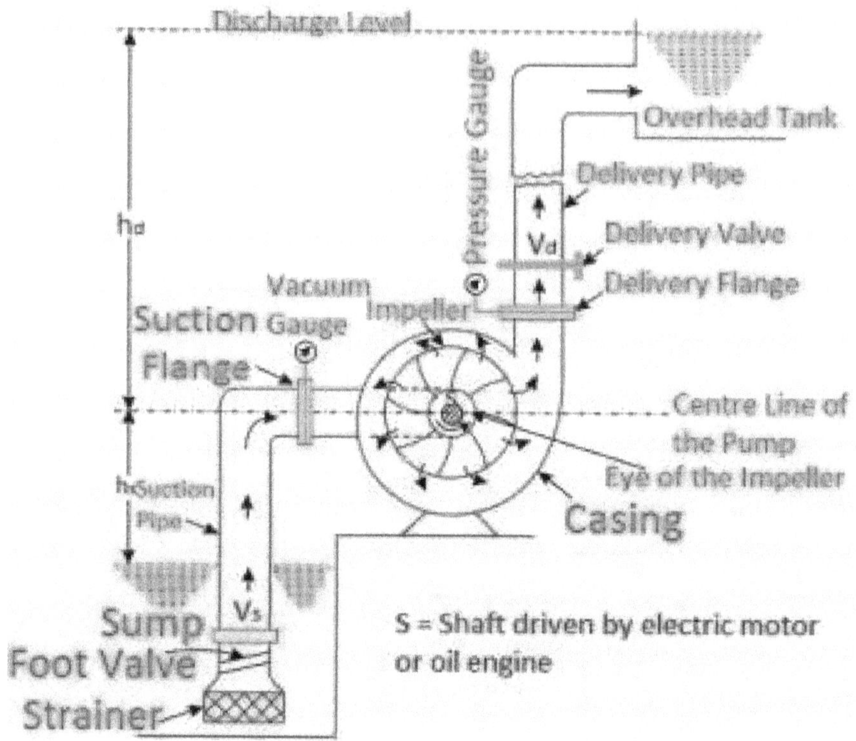

Centrifugal pump

Working of Centrifugal Pump (Step-by-Step)

Priming - Before starting the pump, the casing must be filled with water to remove air (called priming). This is essential for proper functioning.

Motor Starts the Impelle - The impeller rotates at high speed, creating a low-pressure region at the center (eye of the impeller).

Suction of Liquid - Due to the pressure difference, water is drawn from the sump through the suction pipe into the impeller.

Centrifugal Force Action - As water enters the rotating impeller, it is pushed outward by centrifugal force, gaining kinetic energy.

Conversion to Pressure Energy - Water flows into the volute casing, where the kinetic energy is converted into pressure energy due to the gradually increasing cross-section.

Discharge - The pressurized water is then delivered through the delivery pipe to the desired height or location.

The head developed by the pump depends on impeller speed, diameter, and design.Priming is mandatory before starting the pump; otherwise, it will not function properly and may be damaged.

Advantages of Centrifugal Pump

- Simple and compact design
- Easy to install and maintain
- Suitable for large discharge and moderate head
- Can handle clean or slightly dirty liquids

Limitations

- Not suitable for high-head applications
- Requires priming before use
- Efficiency drops at low flow rates

5.2.1 Casing and Impeller

Understanding the types of casings and impellers is important because they directly affect the pump's efficiency, performance, and application. The casing controls the flow and pressure, while the impeller imparts energy to the fluid.

Types of Casings in Centrifugal Pumps

The casing encloses the impeller and helps convert the kinetic energy into pressure energy by gradually decreasing the fluid velocity.

a) Volute Casing

Design: Spiral-shaped casing with increasing cross-sectional area.

Function: Gradually reduces fluid velocity and increases pressure.

Advantage: Minimizes energy loss due to eddies.

Use: Common in standard centrifugal pumps.

Diagram Tip: Show a volute casing with an impeller and expanding spiral passage.

b) Vortex Casing (or Diffuser Casing)

Design: A circular chamber (vortex) is provided between impeller and volute casing.

Function: Reduces loss of kinetic energy and improves efficiency.

Advantage: Smoother flow transition; higher efficiency than plain volute.

Use: Used where energy recovery is important.

c) Casing with Guide Vanes (Diffuser Ring Type)

Design: Vanes (diffuser blades) are fixed around the impeller.

Function: Convert velocity into pressure energy more gradually.

Advantage: Very high efficiency, especially at high flow rates.

Use: High-efficiency industrial or multistage pumps.

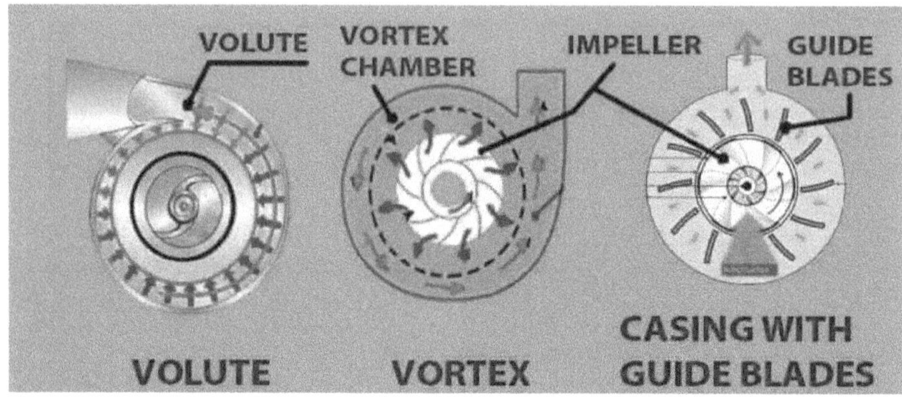

Types of casing

The impeller is the rotating component that imparts kinetic energy to the fluid. Based on blade design and flow direction, impellers are classified as follows:

a) Closed Impeller

Blades enclosed between two discs

Most efficient; used in clear fluids

b) Semi-Open Impeller

One side open; one side shrouded

Handles slightly dirty water or suspended solids

c) Open Impeller

No shroud; blades exposed

Used for slurry, wastewater, or viscous fluids

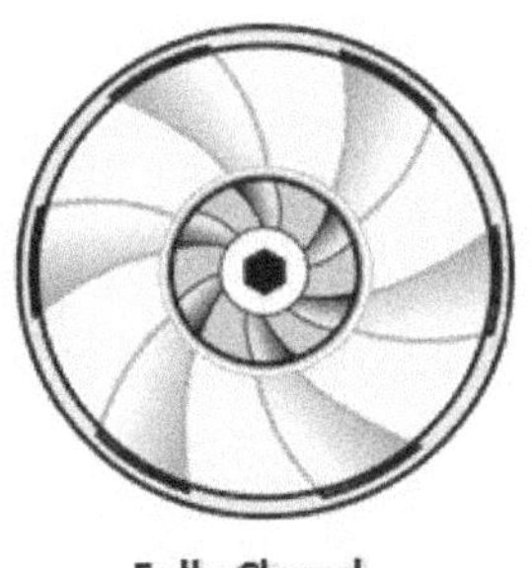

Types of impeller

5.2.2 Concept of Multistage Centrifugal Pump

Introduction

In many practical situations, a single-stage centrifugal pump is not enough to meet the required high head or high discharge. To overcome this, engineers use a multistage centrifugal pump, which connects multiple impellers in series or parallel within a single pump casing.

A multistage centrifugal pump is a pump that contains two or more impellers, mounted on the same shaft, operating in series (for high head) or parallel (for high discharge).

Why Use Multistage Pumps?

- To generate higher heads (pressure) than what a single impeller can produce.
- To achieve higher flow rates by operating impellers in parallel.
- To increase efficiency and reduce pump size for high-head applications.

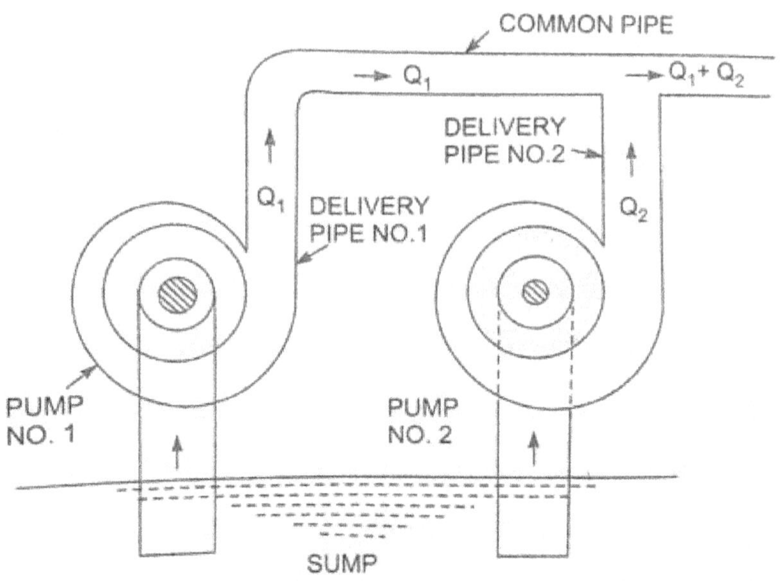

Multistage centrifugal pump

Working Principle :

Each impeller in a multistage pump works just like in a single-stage pump, Water enters the first impeller, gains velocity and pressure. It is passed to the second impeller, where the process repeats. This continues through all impellers, with each stage adding energy to the fluid.

Applications of Multistage Pumps

- Boiler feed pumps (very high-pressure water feeding)
- High-rise buildings and fire-fighting systems
- Water supply systems requiring long-distance or high elevation lift
- Reverse osmosis systems and desalination plants
- Mine dewatering at great depths

5.2.3 Primming and its method

Introduction

Before starting a centrifugal pump, it is essential to ensure that the pump casing and suction pipe are completely filled with liquid (usually water). This process is known as priming. Priming is necessary because centrifugal pumps cannot pump air — they rely on a pressure difference created by the impeller, which only works if the pump is filled with liquid.

Definition of Priming

Priming is the process of filling the pump casing and suction pipe with the liquid to be pumped, before starting the centrifugal pump.Without priming, the impeller will rotate in air, and the pump will fail to generate suction, leading to dry running and damage.

Why Priming is Necessary

A centrifugal pump cannot create self-suction because air has very low density. If air is present, it causes air binding and no flow condition. Proper priming ensures, Continuous flow of water, Avoidance of pump damage, Efficient operation.

Methods of Priming

Manual Priming - Water is poured manually into the pump casing through a plug.

Priming with Foot Valve - A foot valve is installed at the suction pipe end to retain water between uses.

Priming by Vacuum Pump - Air is removed using a vacuum pump connected to the pump casing.

Priming by Jet Pump (Ejector) - A high-speed water jet creates a vacuum to draw water into the casing.

Self-Priming Pumps - Pump is specially designed to re-prime itself automatically after initial filling.

Precautions During Priming

- Ensure air is completely removed from casing and suction pipe.
- Always close the delivery valve during priming to avoid backflow.
- Do not run the pump without liquid — it may cause overheating or seal failure.

5.2.4 Work Done by Centrifugal Pump, Manometric Head, and Efficiencies

Work Done by the Impeller on Water

In a centrifugal pump, the impeller imparts energy to the water mainly in the form of kinetic energy and pressure energy. This energy is transferred from the rotating impeller to the liquid.

Euler's Equation for Pumps:

$$\text{Work done per unit weight of water} = \frac{1}{g}(V_{w2}u_2 - V_{w1}u_1)$$

Vw2 = Whirl velocity of water at outlet

Vw1 = Whirl velocity of water at inlet (often zero)

u2, u1 = Peripheral velocities at outlet and inlet

g = Acceleration due to gravity (9.81 m/s²)

Manometric Head (H)

Definition:

The manometric head is the total head developed by the pump between the pump inlet and the pump outlet. It represents the actual gain in head (or energy) by the liquid as it passes through the pump.

$$H_m = \frac{P}{\rho g} + \frac{V^2}{2g} + z$$

P = Pressure

ρ = Density of fluid

V = Velocity

z = Elevation head

Power Calculations

a. Water Power (Output Power):

$$P_w = \rho g Q H_m$$

ρ = Density of water (1000 kg/m³)
g = Acceleration due to gravity (9.81 m/s²)
Q = Discharge (m³/s)
Hm = Manometric head (m)

b. Shaft Power (Input to Pump Shaft):

$$P_s = \frac{2\pi NT}{60}$$

N = Speed in rpm
T = Torque in Nm

Efficiencies of a Centrifugal Pump
a. Manometric Efficiency (η)

$$\eta_{man} = \frac{gH_m}{V_{w2}u_2}$$

This measures how effectively the impeller converts energy into head.

b. Mechanical Efficiency (η)

$$\eta_{mech} = \frac{\text{Power at Impeller}}{\text{Shaft Power}} = \frac{P_i}{P_s}$$

It considers mechanical losses in the pump like bearing and friction.

c. Overall Efficiency (η)

$$\eta_o = \frac{\text{Water Power}}{\text{Shaft Power}} = \frac{\rho g Q H_m}{P_s}$$

It is the product of manometric and mechanical efficiency

Sample numericals

Q. A centrifugal pump delivers 30 liters per second of water against a manometric head of 25 m. The input power to the pump shaft is 10 kW. Calculate:

a) Water power (output power)

b) Overall efficiency of the pump

Given:

Discharge, Q=30 L/s = 0.03 m3/s

Manometric head, Hm = 25 m

Shaft power, Ps = 10 kW = 10,000 W

Density of water, ρ=1000 kg/m3

g=9.81 m/s2

a) Water Power (Output Power)

$$P_w = \rho g Q H_m$$

$$P_w = 1000 \times 9.81 \times 0.03 \times 25 = 7357.5 \, W = 7.36 \, kW$$

b) Overall Efficiency

$$\eta_o = \frac{P_w}{P_s} = \frac{7357.5}{10,000} = 0.73575 = 73.58\%$$

Q. A centrifugal pump delivers water with a manometric head of 20 m. The impeller diameter is 40 cm and it rotates at 1200 rpm. The whirl velocity at outlet is 15 m/s. Calculate the manometric efficiency of the pump.

Given:

Hm=20 m

Impeller diameter, D=0.4 m

Speed, N=1200 rpm

Vw2=15 m/s

g=9.81 m/s2

Step 1: Calculate Tangential Velocity at Outlet (u_2)

$$u_2 = \frac{\pi DN}{60} = \frac{\pi \times 0.4 \times 1200}{60} = 25.13\,\text{m/s}$$

Step 2: Manometric Efficiency

$$\eta_{man} = \frac{gH_m}{V_{w2}u_2} = \frac{9.81 \times 20}{15 \times 25.13} = \frac{196.2}{376.95} = 0.5205 = 52.05\%$$

Manometric Efficiency = 52.05%

5.3 Reciprocating Pump

Introduction

A reciprocating pump is a positive displacement pump that delivers a fixed volume of fluid with every stroke. Unlike centrifugal pumps, which impart energy continuously, reciprocating pumps trap a certain amount of fluid and push it forward by piston movement. These pumps are ideal for high-pressure, low-flow applications like boiler feedwater, hydraulic systems, and small-scale irrigation.

Definition

A reciprocating pump is a positive displacement pump in which a piston or plunger reciprocates (moves back and forth) inside a cylinder to draw and discharge fluid.

Main Components of a Reciprocating Pump

Cylinder - Houses the piston and holds the working fluid

Piston or Plunger - Moves back and forth to create suction and discharge

Crank and Connecting Rod - Converts rotary motion of shaft into reciprocating motion

Suction Pipe - Draws fluid from source to pump

Suction Valve - Allows fluid to enter the cylinder during suction stroke

Delivery Pipe - Sends fluid to required location

Delivery Valve - Allows fluid to exit the cylinder during delivery stroke

Air Vessel (optional) - Reduces pressure fluctuations and smoothens flow

Working Principle

The reciprocating pump operates on the principle of positive displacement — fluid is mechanically forced in and out of the pump chamber by a piston or plunger.

The motion is divided into two strokes:

a) Suction Stroke (Piston moves away from the cylinder head)

The piston moves backward inside the cylinder.

This creates a low-pressure (vacuum) zone.

The suction valve opens, and fluid is drawn into the cylinder from the sump or tank.

b) Delivery Stroke (Piston moves toward the cylinder head)

The piston moves forward and compresses the fluid.

The suction valve closes due to pressure rise.

The delivery valve opens, and the fluid is pushed into the delivery pipe.

The reciprocating pump operates on the principle of positive displacement — fluid is mechanically forced in and out of the pump chamber by a piston or plunger.

The motion is divided into two strokes:

Applications

- Boiler feed pumps
- Chemical dosing systems
- High-pressure water jet cleaning
- Small-scale irrigation

- Oil drilling and mining

Advantages

- High pressure delivery
- Accurate and fixed discharge
- Self-priming (can lift water without external priming)
- Suitable for viscous or chemical fluids

Limitations

- Low discharge compared to centrifugal pumps
- Pulsating flow (unless air vessel used)
- Complex design and higher maintenance
- Not suitable for high-discharge needs

5.3.1 *Theoretical Discharge, Slip, and Efficiency of Reciprocating Pumps*

Theoretical Discharge of Reciprocating Pump

The theoretical discharge is the ideal volume of fluid that the pump should deliver without any losses. It depends on the size of the cylinder and the number of strokes per second.

a. Single-Acting Reciprocating Pump

In a single-acting pump, the piston pushes fluid during one stroke only (usually forward stroke).

$$Q_{th} = \frac{A \cdot L \cdot N}{60} \quad (\text{in m}^3/\text{s})$$

A = Area of piston $= \pi D2/4$ (in m²)
L = Stroke length (in m)
N = Speed of crank (in rpm)

b. Double-Acting Reciprocating Pump

In a double-acting pump, both strokes (forward and backward) deliver water.

$$Q_{th} = \frac{2 \cdot A \cdot L \cdot N}{60}$$

Sometimes a small correction is applied to account for rod area in one side of the piston.

Actual Discharge of Pump

Due to leakage, valve delay, or slip, the actual volume delivered by the pump is less than the theoretical discharge.

Qact = Actual volume of water delivered (measured experimentally)

Slip of the Pump

Slip is the difference between theoretical and actual discharge

Slip = Qth–Qact

Efficiency of Reciprocating Pump

Volumetric Efficiency :

$$\eta_v = \frac{Q_{act}}{Q_{th}} \times 100$$

Indicates how effectively the pump delivers fluid compared to its ideal capacity.

- Ideal case: ηv = 100%
- Real case: Usually 80–95%, depending on speed, wear, and maintenance.

Sample numericals

Q. A single-acting reciprocating pump has a cylinder diameter of 200 mm and a stroke length of 300 mm. It runs at 50 rpm. The actual discharge is measured as 0.0014 m³/s. Calculate:

a) Theoretical discharge

b) Slip

c) Volumetric efficiency

Given:

Diameter, D = 200 mm = 0.2 m

Stroke length, L = 300 mm = 0.3 m

Speed, N = 50 rpm

Actual discharge, Qact=0.0014 m3/s

a) Theoretical Discharge:

$$A = \frac{\pi D^2}{4} = \frac{\pi (0.2)^2}{4} = 0.0314 \, \text{m}^2$$

$$Q_{th} = \frac{A \cdot L \cdot N}{60} = \frac{0.0314 \cdot 0.3 \cdot 50}{60} = 0.00785 \, \text{m}^3/s$$

b) Slip:

$$\text{Slip} = Q_{th} - Q_{act} = 0.00785 - 0.0014 = 0.00645 \, \text{m}^3/s$$

c) Volumetric Efficiency:

$$\eta_v = \frac{Q_{act}}{Q_{th}} \times 100 = \frac{0.0014}{0.00785} \times 100 = 17.83\%$$

Theoretical Discharge = 0.00785 m³/s

Slip = 0.00645 m³/s

Volumetric Efficiency = 17.83%

Q. A double-acting reciprocating pump runs at 80 rpm. Theoretical discharge is calculated as 0.0045 m³/s, and actual discharge is 0.0042 m³/s. Find:

a) Slip

b) Percentage slip

c) Volumetric efficiency

Given:

Qth=0.0045 m3/s

Qact=0.0042 m3/s

a) Slip:

$$\text{Slip} = \text{Qth} - \text{Qact} = 0.0045 - 0.0042 = 0.0003 \, m3/s$$

b) Percentage Slip:

$$\%\text{Slip} = 0.0003 \times 100 \, / \, 0.0045 = 6.67\%$$

c) Volumetric Efficiency:

$$\eta v = \text{Qact} \times 100 / \text{Qth} = 0.0042 \times 100 \, / \, 0.0045 = 93.33\%$$

Slip = 0.0003 m³/s

% Slip = 6.67%

Volumetric Efficiency = 93.33%

Glossary

1. Fluid – A substance that can flow and has no fixed shape, such as liquids and gases.

2. Viscosity – A measure of a fluid's resistance to flow.

3. Density – Mass per unit volume of a fluid, usually expressed in kg/m³.

4. Pressure – Force exerted per unit area by a fluid.

5. Bernoulli's Theorem – States that in a flowing fluid, the total energy (pressure + kinetic + potential) remains constant.

6. Continuity Equation – Expresses conservation of mass: A1V1=A2V2 , where A is area and V is velocity.

7. Laminar Flow – Smooth and orderly flow of fluid in parallel layers.

8. Turbulent Flow – Irregular and chaotic fluid flow with eddies and swirls.

9. Reynolds Number – A dimensionless number used to predict flow type (laminar or turbulent).

10. Venturimeter – A device used to measure the flow rate of a fluid using pressure difference.

11. Notch – An opening in a tank or channel used to measure flow, often triangular or rectangular.

12. Jet – A stream of fluid discharged from an orifice or nozzle.

13. Impact of Jet – The force exerted by a jet of fluid when it strikes a surface.

14. Pelton Wheel – An impulse turbine used for high-head, low-flow applications.

15. Francis Turbine – A reaction turbine used for medium head and discharge.

16. Kaplan Turbine – An axial flow reaction turbine for low head and high flow.

17. Draft Tube – A diverging tube that reduces the velocity and increases the pressure of water leaving the turbine.

18. Cavitation – The formation and collapse of vapor bubbles in a fluid, which can damage turbine parts.

19. Pump – A machine used to move fluids from one place to another by increasing pressure.

20. Centrifugal Pump – A rotodynamic pump that uses a rotating impeller to move fluid.

21. Reciprocating Pump – A positive displacement pump that uses a piston to push fluid.

22. Priming – The process of filling a pump casing with liquid before starting to prevent air-locking.

23. Manometric Head – The actual head developed by the pump, considering losses.

24. Slip – The difference between theoretical and actual discharge in a reciprocating pump.

25. Hydraulic Ram – A pump that uses water hammer effect to lift water without external power.

About the Author

Mr. Dainikkumar Vasantbhai Savalia is currently serving as an Assistant Professor in the Department of Mechanical Engineering at Parul University, Gujarat, India. With a solid academic foundation, he holds a Bachelor's degree in Mechanical Engineering, a Master of Technology in Thermal Engineering, and is presently pursuing a Ph.D. in Thermal Engineering.

He has a passion for teaching core mechanical subjects and has several years of experience guiding diploma and undergraduate students. His research interests lie in nanofluids, heat transfer enhancement, and sustainable cooling technologies, and he has presented and published papers in reputed national and international conferences.

Mr. Dainikkumar Vasantbhai Savalia also actively contributes to academic administration, currently managing many portfolios of the university. His student-focused approach and ability to simplify complex concepts make him a popular and respected educator.

This book, Fluid Mechanics and Hydraulic Machines, has been specially written to meet the needs of Diploma Mechanical Engineering students, with a focus on clarity, step-by-step explanations, solved numericals, and industry-oriented understanding.

"Teaching is not about delivering information, but about inspiring understanding."
– Mr. Dainikkumar Vasantbhai Savalia